WRITERS AND THEIR WORK

ISOBEL ARMSTRONG
General Editor

WILLIAM MAKEPEACE THACKERAY

WILLIAM MAKEPEACE THACKERAY

WILLIAM MAKEPEACE THACKERAY

Richard Salmon

NORTHCOTE

BRITISH COUNCIL

ATLANTIC
PUBLISHERS & DISTRIBUTORS (P) LTD

This edition is published by

ATLANTIC
PUBLISHERS & DISTRIBUTORS (P) LTD
7/22, Ansari Road, Darya Ganj, New Delhi-110 002
Tel: 40775252, 23273880, 23275880, 23280451; Fax: +91-11-23285873
E-mail: orders@atlanticbooks.com; Web: www.atlanticbooks.com

By arrangement with
Northcote House Publishers Ltd
Horndon House, Horndon, Tavistock, Devon, PL19 9NQ,
United Kingdom. (T)+44(0)1822 810066; (F)+44(0)1822 810034
(E) northcote.house@virgin.net and (W) www.northcotehouse.co.uk
The *Writers and their Work* series is published in association with the British Council.

First Indian Reprint 2010
First published in 2005 by Northcote House Publishers Ltd

ISBN 978-81-269-1322-0

For Sale in the Indian sub-continent only. Not for export elsewhere.

British Library Cataloguing-in-Publication Data
A catalogue record for this book is available from the British Library

Typeset by TW Typesetting, Plymouth, Devon
Printed in India at Nice Printing Press, A-33/3A, Site-IV,
Industrial Area, Sahibabad, Ghaziabad, U.P.

Contents

Acknowledgements vi

Biographical Outline vii

Abbreviations and References x

Introduction: The Antiquary of the Future 1

1 Writing for the Day: Thackeray and the Literary Trade 12

2 Allegory and the World of Things 35

3 Truthful Illusions: Thackeray's Realism 59

4 Historiography and Historical Fiction 84

Notes 109

Select Bibliography 113

Index 117

Acknowledgements

My thanks, as always, to Isobel Armstrong for her advice and encouragement during the conception and writing of this book. I am very grateful, also, to Alistair Stead for his scrupulous reading of the final manuscript, and to Jane Moody and Hugh Stevens for giving me the opportunity to develop part of the argument of Chapter 2 for a guest lecture at the University of York in the summer of 2001.

Biographical Outline

1811 Born in Calcutta, 18 July.

1815 Death of father, Richmond Thackeray, on 13 September.

1816–7 Sent to England for schooling. Mother, Anne Becher, marries Henry Carmichael-Smyth.

1822 Enters Charterhouse School in London.

1828 Leaves Charterhouse.

1829 Matriculation at Trinity College, Cambridge, where he writes for student journals.

1830 Leaves Cambridge without taking a degree. Tours Germany, where he meets Goethe.

1831 Enters the Middle Temple (London) as a law student.

1833 Invests money in a literary periodical, the *National Standard*, of which he becomes owner and editor.

1834 Loss of private fortune and financial failure of the *National Standard*.

1834–6 Studies art in London and Paris.

1836 Marriage to Isabella Shawe on 20 August. Employed as Paris correspondent for the *Constitutional*.

1837 Birth of first daughter, Anne, on 9 June. Serialization of *The Memoirs of Mr Charles J. Yellowplush* in *Fraser's Magazine* (November 1837–August 1838).

1838 Birth of second daughter, Jane, on 9 July.

1839 Death of Jane Thackeray on 14 March. Serialization of *Catherine* in *Fraser's Magazine* (May 1839–February 1840).

1840 Birth of third daughter, Harriet, on 28 May. Publication of *The Paris Sketch Book* (July).

1841 Serialization of 'The History of Samuel Titmarsh and the Great Hoggarty Diamond' in *Fraser's Magazine* (September–December).

1842 Isabella Thackeray placed in private asylum at Chaillot in France, suffering from severe mental illness. Tours Ireland from July to November.

1843 Publication of *The Irish Sketch Book* (May).

1844 Serialization of *The Luck of Barry Lyndon* in *Fraser's Magazine* (January to December). Tour of the Mediterranean and Near East (August–October).

1845 Isabella moved to private nursing care in Camberwell (London), where she stays throughout the remainder of his life.

1846 Publication *of Notes of a Journey from Cornhill to Grand Cairo* (January). First number of *The Snobs of England* appears in *Punch* (March).

1847 Begins publication of *Vanity Fair* in twenty monthly instalments (January). Last number of *The Snobs of England* (February). Publication of *Punch's Prize Novelists* (later retitled *Novels by Eminent Hands)* from April to October.

1848 Last number of *Vanity Fair* (July). Begins publication of *The History of Pendennis* in twenty-three monthly instalments (November).

1849 Publication of *Pendennis* disrupted by serious illness (September–December).

1850 Last number of *Pendennis* (November).

1851 Delivers a series of six lectures on 'The English Humourists of the Eighteenth Century' in London (May–July). Resigns from *Punch* (December).

1852 Lectures on 'The English Humourists' in Scotland and northern England. Publication of *The History of Henry Esmond* in three volumes (October). Embarks on lecture tour of the United States (October).

1853 Returns from America (May). Begins publication of *The Newcomes* in twenty-four monthly instalments (October).

1855 Last number of *The Newcomes* (August). Embarks on second tour of the United States, lecturing on 'The Four Georges' (October).

1856 Returns from America (May). Lectures on 'The Four Georges' in Scotland and northern England (November–December).

1857 Lecturing in England and Scotland (January–May). Stands unsuccessfully as a parliamentary candidate for Oxford (July). Begins publication of *The Virginians* in twenty-four monthly instalments (November).

1858 Involved in the 'Garrick Club Affair', a dispute with Edmund Yates and Charles Dickens (June–July).

1859 Appointed editor of the *Cornhill Magazine.* Last number of *The Virginians* (October).

1860 First issue of the *Cornhill Magazine* (January). Publication of *Lovel the Widower* (January–June), *The Four Georges* (July–October) and *The Roundabout Papers* (January 1860–November 1863) in the *Cornhill Magazine.*

1861 Begins serialization of *The Adventures of Philip* in the *Cornhill Magazine* (January).

1862 Resigns editorship of the *Cornhill Magazine* (March). Last number of *Philip* (August).

1863 Begins writing *Denis Duval,* published posthumously in the *Cornhill Magazine* (March–June 1864). Last number of *The Roundabout Papers* (November). Dies on 24 December and is buried in Kensal Green cemetery.

Abbreviations and References

BL	*The Memoirs of Barry Lyndon, Esq.*, ed. Andrew Sanders (World's Classics; Oxford: Oxford University Press, 1984)
CH	Geoffrey Tillotson and Donald Hawes (eds.), *Thackeray: The Critical Heritage* (London: Routledge and Kegan Paul, 1968)
HE	*The History of Henry Esmond, Esq.*, ed. Donald Hawes (World's Classics; Oxford: Oxford University Press, 1991)
LPP	*The Letters and Private Papers of William Makepeace Thackeray*, ed. Gordon N. Ray (4 vols.; London: Oxford University Press, 1945–6)
NC	*The Newcomes: Memoirs of a Most Respectable Family*, ed. Andrew Sanders (World's Classics; Oxford: Oxford University Press, 1995)
P.	*The History of Pendennis*, ed. John Sutherland (World's Classics; Oxford: Oxford University Press, 1994)
VF	*Vanity Fair: A Novel without a Hero*, ed. John Sutherland (World's Classics; Oxford: Oxford University Press, 1983)
WMT	*The Biographical Edition of The Works of William Makepeace Thackeray* (13 vols.: London: Smith, Elder, & Co., 1898–9)

Introduction: The Antiquary of the Future

This book begins, as it ends, by considering William Makepeace Thackeray's location in time. Time, and its inscription into the narrative form of history, is not only one of the persistent preoccupations of Thackeray's writing, as I suggest in a later chapter, but it is also, of course, the medium in which his critical reputation (like that of any other writer) has evolved. Out of all the canonical Victorian novelists, there is perhaps none whose status amongst both academic literary critics and non-academic readers has shifted so radically over the past 150 years as that of Thackeray. For most educated readers of the latter half of the nineteenth century, Thackeray was, unquestionably, one of the great novelists, as well as one of the great cultural and moral authorities, of his age. His rivalry with Charles Dickens for the mantle of greatest living novelist in the English language was, for a period of more than a decade in the middle of the century, accepted as a truism by Victorian reviewers. Charlotte Brontë, George Eliot, and Anthony Trollope are amongst the more notable of his contemporary readers to have ranked Thackeray higher than Dickens in this contest – a judgement that stands in stark contrast to their respective positions within the bookshops and university syllabuses of the early twenty-first century.

The Victorians' veneration of Thackeray (although, of course, it was by no means universal) can be said to have begun with Brontë's famous Preface to the second edition of *Jane Eyre* (1847), in which she dedicates her text to the author of *Vanity Fair*, a novel whose publication in serial form over the course of the preceding *year* had not yet reached its conclusion. Here, Thackeray was eulogized for possessing 'an intellect profounder and more unique than his contemporaries have yet recognized', and heralded as 'the first social regenerator of the day – as the very master of that working corps who would restore to rectitude the warped system of things'.[1] Though Brontë's admiration for Thackeray's power as a satirist and reformative social critic was to be somewhat tempered by a more extensive acquaintance with his work, it was broadly endorsed in many subsequent assessments of his literary achievement. In a letter to her publisher John Blackwood, written in June 1857, for instance, George Eliot responded to the criticism of having adopted a 'Thackerayan view of human nature' in her own fiction by declaring that 'I am not conscious of being in any way a disciple of his, unless it constitute discipleship to think him, as I suppose the majority of people with any intellect do, on the whole the most powerful of living novelists'.[2] A similar judgement was expressed by Thackeray's most self-conscious disciple, Anthony Trollope, who did 'not hesitate to name Thackeray the first' in a survey of contemporary English novelists conducted in his *Autobiography* (1883): according to Trollope, Thackeray's 'knowledge of human nature was supreme, and his characters stand out as human beings, with a force and a truth which has not, I think, been within the reach of any other English novelist in any period'.[3]

Leaving aside the tendentiousness of literary rankings, what such comments reveal about Thackeray's Victorian reputation is its association with intellectual authority and a certain cultural prestige. Eliot's assumption that Thackeray's most appreciative audience comprised of 'people with any intellect' was commonly held during his lifetime, and particularly evident in comparisons with the more popular Dickens. The intellectual 'power', 'profundity', and 'truthfulness' that many of his contemporaries, even those critical of his work, saw in Thackeray can, on the one hand, be ascribed to his perceived occupancy of the role of cultural 'sage', a figure emerging out of the widely held Victorian conception of the moral and social responsibility of the writer. Although he sought to disclaim any affinity with the archetypal Victorian sages (such as Thomas Carlyle), it is a posture that his authorial voice can, at times, appear to cultivate. On the other hand, these qualities may be related, implicitly, to a perceived class identity, which elevates Thackeray above the 'ordinary' rank of novelist – fiction being viewed as an inferior, somewhat disreputable, genre for much of the nineteenth century. In the standard mid-Victorian comparison between Thackeray and Dickens, the former emerges as a writer who appeals not only to the intellectual reader in particular, but, just as specifically, to an ideal of middle-class literary decorum. This perception was a response not so much to content as it was to form. As G. H. Lewes observed in a review of *The History of Pendennis* (1848–50), Thackeray's literary style was recognizable as 'essentially the style of a gentleman': its principal characteristic being that 'it is not a style in the vulgar sense of the word; that is to say, it is not a *trick*', unlike, presumably, the ostentatious writing of his literary and social inferiors (*CH* 106). This, once again, is a surprisingly common Victorian explanation of Thackeray's cultural value, which has subsequently lost all currency (and even visibility) within critical discourse. Thackeray himself, however, was conscious of a tension between his inherited social status as a 'gentleman' and his chosen profession of authorship, with its potentially degrading association with commerce, and appears to have felt an ambivalent attraction to both sides of the divide.

It is all the more surprising to learn that Thackeray's Victorian reputation was, in part, founded upon the qualities of his style (albeit on transparently ideological grounds), and not solely as a satirist, sage, or cultural critic, since it was on the basis of literary form, primarily, that his reputation began to decline in the early to mid-twentieth century. The charge of *formlessness* began to pervade critical responses to Thackeray's fiction from the publication of Henry James's 1908 preface to the 'New York' edition of his novel *The Tragic Muse*, in which *The Newcomes* (1853–5) is cited alongside works by Tolstoy and Alexandre Dumas as representative of an 'accidental and ... arbitrary' method of novelistic composition, resulting in the production of 'large loose baggy monsters'.[4] Unfortunately, for Thackeray's reputation, the phrase 'large loose baggy monsters' became a pejorative term with which his name remained synonymous during several decades of the mid-twentieth century, when a school of formalist criticism, explicitly influenced by the opposing Jamesian principle of 'organic form', dominated Anglo-American criticism on the novel. Alongside this common tendency to depreciate the inorganic formal and artistic design of Thackeray's novels was a growing recognition, amongst other critics, of their stature within the nineteenth-century European tradition of realist fiction. For the Marxist Georg Lukács, writing in the late 1930s, Thackeray is an 'outstanding critical realist', whose insight into the sociohistorical character of his era can be ranked with that of Scott, Balzac, and Flaubert.[5] It was also the case that Thackeray's reputation as a satirical commentator upon normative aspects of Victorian culture and ideology insulated him, to some extent, against the anti-Victorian reaction of the early twentieth century. Nevertheless, by mid-century, even sympathetic critics of Thackeray were forced to acknowledge the uncertainty surrounding his predominant critical status. In the preface to his 1954 study *Thackeray the Novelist*, Geoffrey Tillotson, for example, assumes that 'at the present day the place of Thackeray's novels in the regard of Englishmen, and perhaps also of Americans, has its interest for any historian of literary reputations', whilst complaining that 'most of the critics whose work achieves print dislike or slight them'.[6]

Even the popular interest, taken for granted by Tillotson, came to seem increasingly tenuous in the latter half of the century. Amongst the flurry of notable critical studies of Thackeray published during the 1970s, a perception of his relative inaccessibility to modern readers emerges as a recognizable trend. In *The Exposure of Luxury: Radical Themes in Thackeray*, published in 1972, Barbara Hardy notes how 'it seems impossible to take for granted either the extent or the depth of knowledge' of his writings in comparison with that of Hardy, Eliot, or Dickens, whereas in *Thackeray: Prodigal Genius* (1977) John Carey goes so far as to accept George Orwell's verdict (expressed in 1944) on the virtual unreadability of the later novels, a view that corresponds to the growing cultural invisibility of works such as *Henry Esmond* (1852), *The Newcomes*, and *The Virginians* (1857–9).[7] The basis of both academic and 'popular' knowledge of Thackeray has, in recent years, come increasingly to rest upon *Vanity Fair*, the one text to have survived virtually unscathed from the precipitous decline in his twentieth-century reputation. Although, since its original publication, *Vanity Fair* has always maintained a prominent position within Thackeray's *oeuvre,* the virtually exclusive prominence that it currently occupies must be seen as a recent critical phenomenon: for many Victorian readers, the achievement of *Vanity Fair* was at least equalled, if not surpassed, by that of *Henry Esmond* and *The Newcomes.* This observation, of course, does not in itself constitute an argument for the restoration of these texts to their former critical status or cultural familiarity. One of the purposes of this book is, however, to introduce readers to a much broader range of Thackeray's writings than is customarily available, as a result both of the narrow concentration of recent criticism on *Vanity Fair* and of the fact that many of his texts are now no longer easily obtainable in print. If Thackeray is still conventionally regarded as one of the canonical Victorian novelists, his is a canonicity now just as likely to be neglected as some of the 'neglected' writers whose novels have recently entered into the academic canon of Victorian studies.

To account fully for the vicissitudes of Thackeray's cultural status during the twentieth century would require a more thorough examination of the changing contexts of critical reception than the 'scope of this brief, introductory survey allows. Some speculative suggestions as to the basis of the supposed inaccessibility of his writing, however, may be useful, at this juncture, as a way of prefacing some of the issues raised in later chapters. One practical obstacle to the easy assimilation of Thackeray's fiction by present-day readers, it might be thought, is the sheer, unremitting length of almost all of his novels from *Vanity Fair* onwards. Although, of course, this argument may be countered by the examples of Eliot and Dickens, whose later and longer novels are, if anything, more widely appreciated now than at any time in the past, Thackeray's reputation has unquestionably suffered from the peculiar exigencies of the dominant mid-Victorian mode of novel production. The 'large loose baggy monsters' of mid-Victorian fiction are the direct consequence of a system of serial publication, under which novels were initially designed to be read either through the medium of periodicals or in separate 'part-issue' form. The process of serialization typically extended over a period of up to two years, during which time the act of writing and the event of publication became more or less simultaneous. With the single exception of *Henry Esmond*, all Thackeray's full-length novels were originally composed and published in serial form, and the necessarily improvisational aspect of this method of narrative construction has often attracted adverse commentary. Even some sympathetic critics, such as John Sutherland, have characterized Thackeray's working practice as 'casual' and unpremeditated,[8] in tacit agreement with the Jamesian charge of formlessness. But a more accurate conception of this practice would be as an essentially journalistic mode of production, to which Thackeray was habituated by his early apprenticeship as a writer for periodicals such as *Fraser's Magazine* and *Punch*. The serial form of his novels contributes not only to their exorbitant length, but to an impression of generic indeterminacy that can be traced to their origins in the journalistic culture of the 1830s and 1840s. For instance, the 'Pen and Pencil Sketches', of which the continuous narrative of *Vanity Fair is* comprised, are, in some ways, a direct extension of the miscellaneous journalistic sketches that Thackeray had produced over the preceding decade. A journalistic absorption in the passing interests of the present moment may also he responsible for infusing Thackeray's fiction with a degree of contemporary cultural specificity that enhances its temporal remoteness from later readers. This cultural specificity is expressed, in formal terms, through his penchant for satire and parody – genres that thrive within the intertextual medium of the periodical, but whose contemporary referents may well be lost when transposed into the permanent form of the book.

Perversely, when Thackeray's writing is not absorbed by the ephemeral present, it often appears preoccupied with an antiquarian reconstruction of the past. Several of his novels – including the very first – *Catherine* (1839) – and the last – *Denis Duval* (1864) – are set in the eighteenth century, a period of history as remote from the Victorians as they are from us. As Andrew Sanders has observed, the prestige that the genre of the historical novel held within the nineteenth century (after the enormous cultural influence of Walter Scott) did not, in general, extend far into the twentieth century.[9] Indeed, the fate of Thackeray's own historical fiction was correctly predicted in Goldwin Smith's review of *The Virginians* published in the *Edinburgh Review* in 1859. Given that Thackeray's fascination with the eighteenth century is largely inspired by Henry Fielding's *contemporary* fictional representations of the period, it is unlikely, Smith deduces, that 'posterity' will revisit the nineteenth-century novels of Thackeray for anything other than representations of his own age (*CH* 289–91). By and large, this assumption holds true. If the material density of Thackeray's immersion in the minutiae of nineteenth-century culture (both Regency and Victorian) can seem opaque to readers of the present day, his equally microscopic attention to the periods of Queen Anne or George II is both even more remote and apparently devoid of the 'authentic' documentary historical value that can be attributed to the former. The virtual disappearance from recent cultural discourse of *Henry Esmond*, a text that Trollope deemed the 'best novel in the English language',[10] is symptomatic of this difficulty.

The best way of beginning to overcome some of these obstacles to our current understanding of Thackeray, however, is not to minimize their significance, but, rather, to become aware of the challenges that they pose to our own critical, aesthetic, and historiographical assumptions. Some of the mint recent criticism on Thackeray, and on Victorian culture in general, helps us to achieve this aim. It is no longer the case, for example, that the theory of the novel is dominated by a Jamesian doctrine of 'organic form', as it was up until the 1960s. The development of post-formalist critical theory, and, to some extent, of postmodernist literary practice, has created the opportunity for a rehabilitation (or, rather, reconceptualization) of the narrative strategies of mid-Victorian fiction. It is possible not only to 'explain' the 'arbitrary and . . . accidental' character of the serial novel by locating it within the original material context of its production and reception, but even to vindicate the aesthetic effects generated by the contingency of its narrative form. Similarly, it is possible to examine Thackeray's very particular brand of 'realism' without simplistically counterposing it against the anti-realist trajectory of twentieth-century fiction: in fact, as I suggest later, Thackeray's critique of fictional illusion is as rigorously sceptical as that of any recent work of postmodern 'meta-fiction'. In short, Thackeray's fiction can be defended against the charge of formlessness, not by abandoning the category of literary form altogether, but, more specifically, by challenging its supposed opposition to an unmediated cultural content, to 'realism' in the naive sense of the word. At the same time, the nature of the 'content' of his fiction can also be reassessed in the light of the recent critical interest in questions of gender, race, and material culture. Since the mid-1980s, some of the most significant work on Thackeray has opened up new areas of enquiry into the historical contexts and cultural politics of his writing, although its effect on the more specialized field of 'Thackeray studies' has yet to be fully realized. Eve Kosofsky Sedgwick's extensive use of Thackeray in her analysis of nineteenth-century codes of homosocial masculinity, Patrick Brantlinger's study of his relationship to imperial ideology (with particular reference to his fascination with India), and Andrew Miller's discussion of commodity culture in *Vanity Fair* and other texts provide good examples of these recent critical preoccupations, some of which have shaped the thinking of the present book.[11]

The broadly historicist assumptions that underpin much of this criticism can be of assistance in providing both a theoretical foundation and an empirical framework for retrieving those elements of Thackeray's writing that appear most forbiddingly specific to the cultural milieu out of which it emerged. From a historicist perspective, it would be merely tautological to criticize Thackeray for failing to transcend the historical difference that separates him from the cultural horizon of later readers: such difference is an inherent feature of the historicity of all literary texts. The populist criterion of 'relevance', now routinely demanded of the cultural products of an earlier age, often arises out of an attempt to abolish this historical difference: to compel the past to gratify the consumerist desires of the present. Against this tendency, it remains important to insist on the value of reading Thackeray's texts precisely *because* of our current estrangement from them. In a passage from *Pendennis*, Thackeray himself suggests a way of conceptualizing the role of the future reader of his texts that supports this possibility. Describing a scene in which Major Pendennis is reading about the latest 'presentations' of society ladies in his morning newspaper, the narrator notes how 'in a further part of the paper their dresses were described, with a precision and in a jargon which will puzzle and amuse the antiquary of future generations' (*P*. 457). The combined puzzlement and amusement felt by the future antiquarian reader of a daily newspaper serves as an apposite metaphor for the peculiar temporal experience of the present-day reader of Thackeray's fiction. In the form of an old newspaper, an image of the quotidian reality of the past survives as if it were still present, just as in much of Thackeray's fiction a journalistic saturation in the concrete particularity of nineteenth-century culture is preserved for the benefit of posterity. Simultaneously distanced from the past and engaged by its ephemeral consciousness of being present, the antiquarian reader approaches the historical text, in both cases, as if it were neither fully alive nor utterly dead. Yet, in another sense, it is Thackeray himself who poses as the 'antiquary of future generations' in this passage. The perspective of futurity is not one that needs to be imposed on his writing retrospectively, or from outside, since it is already inscribed within *Pendennis*, as a proleptic invocation of a future moment of retrospection. In this respect, a purely historicist account of the position of Thackeray's fiction within history seems somewhat inadequate, or even incongruous. Thackeray's own conception of history, as I suggest later, was by no means one of an even, continuous flow of time, in which the present supersedes the past along a linear path of development. In particular, the importance that is attached to memory in many of his narratives cautions the reader against assuming that the past represents an entirely discrete historical moment, uncontaminated by the experience of the present and future; hence, perhaps, the oscillating attraction to the eighteenth and nineteenth centuries, which can be observed both within individual texts and across the whole course of his literary career.

In accordance with the non-linear pattern of Thackeray's historical consciousness (though not simply because of it), the structure of this book avoids a strictly chronological representation of his work and life. The reasons for this decision are as much pragmatic as a matter of principle. By Victorian standards, Thackeray's literary output remains quantitatively slender, and the period of its production relatively brief. During the whole of his career, he completed no more than eight full-length novels, and a span of exactly twenty years separates the publication of his first substantive novel, *The Luck of Barry Lyndon* (1844), from the posthumous publication of *Denis Duval*, a year after his premature death in *1863*. Thus, beyond an approximate division between 'early' and 'later' writings, often demarcated by the watershed publication of *Vanity Fair*, it is not customary to think of Thackeray's career in terms of an elaborate succession of discrete chronological phases. What counts as Thackeray's writing is, of course, not restricted to novels: in addition, he wrote numerous shorter fictional narratives, as well as lectures, sketches, travelogues, and reviews, the majority of which appeared during the earlier, pre-*Vanity Fair* period of the 1830s and 1840s. Much of this miscellaneous material now lies buried within its original periodical form or in the great collected editions of Thackeray's works published during the nineteenth and early twentieth centuries: sharing, to an extent, John Carey's view that it is often of equal or greater interest than some of the more monumental later novels, I have accorded it as much attention as space has allowed.[12] For the sake of enhanced clarity, I have sought to concentrate discussion of Thackeray's earlier writings in Chapters 1 and 2 and of later texts in Chapters 3 and 4. However, the division of chapters within the book is organized primarily on conceptual, rather than chronological, grounds, and there is significant overlap in terms of their attention to individual texts. Chapter 1, 'Writing for the Day', examines Thackeray's conception of the role and cultural status of the writer, with particular emphasis placed upon the formative experience of his early journalistic career. Its aim is to provide an account of the specific material contexts and diverse generic forms of literary-journalistic production, which helped to shape his understanding of the profession – or, in his view, *trade* – of letters. Chapter 2, 'Allegory and the World of Things', proceeds to discuss Thackeray's sensitivity to the material forms of contemporary culture within a broader context of literary representation and social critique. The chapter takes as its focal point *Vanity Fair*, a novel that both satirizes and allegorizes the hegemonic materialism of nineteenth-century bourgeois society, but places it alongside a number of less familiar texts in which the materiality of Thackeray's imagination is embodied in an equally ambivalent form. Chapter 3, 'Truthful Illusions', covers the related, but perhaps more familiar, topic of Thackeray's literary 'realism', the aesthetic manifestation of his anti-idealist and anti-Romantic philosophy. The central texts for this discussion are the three interrelated novels written either about or by the fictive autobiographical persona of Arthur Pendennis: *Pendennis* itself, *The Newcomes*, and *The Adventures of Philip* (1861–2). Finally, in Chapter 4, 'Historiography and Historical Fiction', I return to the question of history by considering Thackeray's contribution to the genre of the historical novel in *Henry Esmond* and *The Virginians*, and, more generally, exploring his increasing preoccupation with the experience of time, memory, ageing, and the past.

The contents of these four chapters do not, of course, exhaust the list of worthwhile subjects of critical debate, which might be compiled from a reading of the totality of Thackeray's work. Other issues, discussed in passing within each of the chapters, could easily have formed its central topic within a conceivable alternative structure: Thackeray's analysis of class and gender, his relationship to traditions of satire and humour, his practice of both visual and literary art, and so on. But neither is the chosen method of organization an intentionally arbitrary or miscellaneous selection of conceptual 'themes'. In accordance with the introductory aims of this series, my purpose has been to provide as wide a coverage of Thackeray's writing as possible, and, thus, to construct a conceptual framework that allows such a breadth of approach without lapsing into the spurious neutrality of a pure critical miscellany. To this end, what unites each of the following chapters is an attempt to identify, and account for, the recurrent aesthetic, cultural, ideological, and material concerns that give shape, in however contradictory or ambiguous a form, to the achieved body of his writing.

1

Writing for the Day: Thackeray and the Literary Trade

Thackeray's literary career was forged within a time when the very notion of the professional 'literary career' was only beginning to be established. During the course of his working life, he was an active contributor to debates on the professionalization of authorship, the expansion of the literary market, and the cultural effects of journalism – debates that encode a distinctively modern apprehension of 'authors' and their 'works'. An important part of what connects us to Thackeray is this fundamental continuity between the emergence of the conditions of a capitalist literary marketplace, alongside the growth of a predominantly bourgeois profession of authorship, in the early-to-mid-nineteenth century and the prevailing structures of literary culture within our own time. But though he is a 'modern' writer in this broad sociohistorical sense, there is, of course, much that seems alien and remote to present-day readers about the particular literary milieu in which Thackeray's texts were produced. Even more than in the case of most Victorian novelists, it is important to temper our reading of Thackeray with an understanding of the differing modes of publication and generic forms through which both his fictional and non-fictional writings were mediated. Most important of all, perhaps, it is necessary to consider the role played by journalism and the periodical press in the formation of Thackeray's sense of identity as a writer, especially during the 1830s and 1840s, the period prior to his first popular success as a novelist.

JOURNALISTIC FORMS

In a contemporary review of Thackeray's semi-autobiographical novel *The History of Pendennis – a* novel that itself traces the entrance of its protagonist into the literary profession by way of journalism – J. W. Kaye characterized the historical moment of its appearance as the 'age of periodical literature'.[1] Within this modern age, Kaye points out, even the most ephemeral kinds of writing can be solidified into the form of 'literary property' via the medium of the periodical press. This is an observation that is borne out by Thackeray's own early experience of journalism, as well as being reflected upon, critically, in his later novels. The vast bulk of Thackeray's literary output from the first decade of his career is essentially ephemeral in character, produced in order to meet the practical exigencies of periodical publication and to exploit opportunities for commercial success within an increasingly buoyant literary marketplace. This period coincides with a considerable expansion of the periodical press in Britain, which can be said to mark the origins of the development of modern 'mass culture'.

Between 1837 and 1847 Thackeray wrote for innumerable periodicals, contributing reviews and correspondence to newspapers such as *The Times*, the *Morning Chronicle*, and the *Calcutta Star*, and a great diversity of texts (including book reviews, art criticism, travel writing, short stories, comic sketches, novels, poems, and drawings) to weekly and monthly magazines of various kinds. Earlier still, he had spent a considerable portion of his private fortune in attempting to establish periodicals of his own: the *National Standard* in 1833–4 and the *Constitutional*, funded chiefly by his father-in-law Henry Carmichael-Smyth, in 1836–7. It is with three magazines in particular, however, that Thackeray's work as a journalist, spanning the whole range of his writing life, is most closely associated. From 1837 to 1844 he was a regular contributor to *Fraser's Magazine for Town and Country*, a monthly Tory journal of fiercely iconoclastic character, edited, most notably, by the Irishman William Maginn. Much of Thackeray's early satirical and parodic writing, including his first two extended works of prose fiction – *Catherine: A Story* (1839–40) and *The Luck of Barry*

Lyndon (1844) – was published in *Fraser's Magazine*, and this periodical context was crucial in shaping both its style and its content. From 1844 onwards the majority of his periodical contributions began to appear in the newly established comic magazine *Punch*, and by the end of the decade he had become one of its most celebrated writers – the publication of a series of comic sketches entitled *The Snobs of England* (1846–7) producing his first popular success. Thackeray's work for *Punch* allowed him to develop his talents as a social satirist, humourist, and parodist of other writers' work, often targeting the same figures as in his earlier writing, despite the more radical political leanings of the new journal. Like *Fraser's Magazine*, *Punch* dealt, initially, in a somewhat scurrilous form of satirical abuse (sometimes xenophobic in content), though it became an increasingly respectable middle-class magazine in later years. So too, in later life, Thackeray attempted to move away from the rather disreputable, bohemian associations of his early journalistic writing, and the third periodical with which his name is closely associated is, accordingly, very different in kind. After a hiatus of some ten years, during which time he had established his reputation as a novelist (as distinct from the other forms of writing to which his early career might conceivably have led), Thackeray returned to the business of journalism, in a substantial way, with the founding of the *Cornhill Magazine* in January *1860*. During the two years in which he edited the *Cornhill*, Thackeray established it as one of the leading examples of a new type of middle-class monthly magazine, aimed specifically at a domestic ('family') readership, which became popular during the 1860s and beyond. In contrast to the almost exclusively masculine satirical manner of *Fraser's Magazine* and *Punch*, the *Cornhill Magazine* might be said to institute a 'feminization' of Victorian journalistic discourse: Thackeray's own personal contributions to the magazine, which encompass serialized fiction, lectures on historical subjects, and a series of editorial reflections under the title of *The Roundabout Papers* (1860–3), are certainly more 'domestic' in orientation than the acerbic satire of his early periodical writing.

In a broader context, however, what is most significant about Thackeray's return to journalism towards the end of his life is not so much the change as the underlying continuity that it reveals in his development as a writer. At the risk of overinterpreting the contingent eventualities of biography, it is tempting to see Thackeray's editorship of the *Cornhill Magazine* as, in some sense, a culmination of his earlier, frustrated ambition to establish a periodical of his own. What is clear, at any rate, is that, for Thackeray, journalism was not the least important of his literary activities, as it may seem to later readers, for whom the status of canonical author is incompatible with a collective mode of production. In an 'age of periodical literature', in which even the form of the novel was bound by the conditions of serial publication, journalism was an activity at the very centre of Victorian cultural life. If the cultural status of the journalist was, at the beginning of the nineteenth century, considered dubiously *declasse*, it was, nevertheless, a role capable of commanding considerable social influence, and became increasingly reputable as the century progressed. Such was the centrality of the periodical to Victorian literary culture, however, that Thackeray was scarcely unique amongst novelists of the period in contributing extensively to them; one could easily demonstrate a similar level of involvement for Dickens, to take another notable example. It is not sufficient, then, simply to enumerate Thackeray's various journalistic activities or associations with particular periodicals: one must also consider the ways in which journalism, as a general medium of cultural production, shaped his understanding of the process of writing and the condition of authorship at a conceptual level.

What distinguishes Thackeray's conception of his status as a journalist from that of many of his contemporaries is an explicit recognition of the inherent temporal conditions and constraints of periodical writing, and a trenchantly materialist refusal to transcend them. Journalism is, by the very nature of its form, ephemeral or transient in affect – intrinsically defined by the regular periodicity of daily, weekly, or monthly publication, as Margaret Beetham has pointed out.[2] As a paradigm of authorship, it sits uncomfortably with the then prevalent Romantic conception of writing as an act that seeks to transcend its originary moment of inscription in order to address a deferred audience, sometimes named 'posterity'. For example, in Thackeray's early journalistic polemics against the contemporary novelist Sir Edward Bulwer-Lytton, it is precisely this conflict between 'Romantic' and journalistic models of authorship that comes to the fore. His first substantial publication for *Fraser's Magazine*, the comic serial entitled *The Memoirs of Mr Charles J. Yellowplush* (1837–8), concludes with an address to Bulwer ('Epistles to the Literati') in which Yellowplush – Thackeray's fictitious footman-persona – mocks the 'Honrabble Barnet's stated ambition of writing for the 'next age', 'looking forward to a future, and fancying that . . . our books are to be immortal' (*WMT* iii. 366, 376). Bulwer's grandiose Romantic rhetoric and self-important assumption of literary 'immortality' are Thackeray's targets here, but implicit within the satire is a serious point about the uncertainty of addressing a readership of the future from the constricted temporal horizon of the present. Several of his critical reviews of the 1840s return to the same point with striking insistence. In 'A Box of Novels' (1844), for instance, Thackeray again cautions against the ambition of writing for 'futurity', enlisting the support of Dickens, Fielding, and Shakespeare as examples of great writers whose work does not seek to transcend the ephemeral concerns of its contemporary moment (*WMT* xiii. *415–16).* While such writing has the capacity to enter into posterity, this will be achieved by virtue of, not in spite of, its contemporary focus. Posterity, Thackeray suggests, does not redeem the injustice of a degraded present time, as is often presupposed in nineteenth-century Romantic aesthetics.

In another review essay, 'A Brother of the Press on the History of a Literary Man, Laman Blanchard, and the Chances of the Literary Profession' (1846), the journalistic context of this debate emerges more explicitly. Thackeray is responding in this review to Bulwer's posthumous memoir of the life of Laman Blanchard, a little-known journalist of the period. Whereas Bulwer had regarded Blanchard's career as evidence of the damaging effects of journalism on modern literary practice, construing him as a symptomatic victim of the cultural dominance of the periodical form, Thackeray insists that there is nothing to be lamented in the obscurity and anonymous toil of Blanchard's career. Thackeray agrees that Blanchard's status is that of a representative literary hack, but proceeds to defend the integrity of this mode of writing against what he sees as Bulwer's idealized iconography of martyred genius. In response to the familiar complaint that 'the world gives up a lamentable portion of its time to fleeting literature', and that 'authors who might be occupied upon great works fritter away their lives in producing endless hasty sketches', he demands to know 'why should not the day have its literature?' (*WMT* xiii. 466–7). Contained within this text, then, is not simply a passive acceptance of the material conditions of periodical production, but the grounds of a principled defence of journalism as an inherently ephemeral mode of writing. Speaking in the egalitarian voice of one of Blanchard's 'Brother[s] of the Press', Thackeray validates the circumscribed career of the literary hack: 'To do your work honestly, to amuse and instruct your reader of to-day, to die when your time comes, and go hence with as clean a breast as may be; may these be all yours and ours, by God's will' (*WMT* xiii. 468). A similar consciousness of the transitory nature of writing informs much of Thackeray's work, and can be found as distinctly in later novels, such as *The Adventures of Philip*, as in the periodical writing produced prior to the achievement of his own considerable literary fame. Thackeray's early experience of journalism, then, can be seen as important in shaping his more general authorial consciousness, producing what might be conceived as an essentially journalistic literary ethics and aesthetics. This, of course, is not to suggest that the 'reader of to-day' is the sole addressee of Thackeray's texts: as I observed in the 'Introduction', an appeal to futurity, mediated through the retrospective stance of memory, is also a characteristic strategy of his narrative fiction, which remains to be considered (in Chapter 4). The effect of periodical publication on the development of Thackeray's writing career, however, needs now to be discussed in terms of more specific questions of literary form and genre.

As a novelist, the genealogy of Thackeray's career can be traced back to his experiments in the genre of the 'sketch', a self-consciously improvisatory form of literary and/or visual journalism that flourished within the popular magazines of the early nineteenth century. It is interesting to note, for example, that the novel for which Thackeray is most famous – *Vanity*

Fair: A Novel without a Hero (1848) – was published under a different subtitle in its original serial form: *Vanity Fair: Pen and Pencil Sketches of English Society* (1847–8). The shift from *Pen and Pencil Sketches* to A *Novel* implies, amongst other things, a distinction between the singular and achieved totality of book publication and the plurality and provisionality that characterizes the separate, but interconnected, numbers of a serial. In an essay on Thackeray's practice as an illustrator of his own fiction, Stephen Canham has suggested that the 'pencil sketches' of *Vanity Fair* are, indeed, sketchy in character – designed as momentary impressions of character or scene, which are left deliberately unfinished.[3] This provisional aspect of the visual form of the sketch presumably serves as a model for what Thackeray was also seeking to achieve with the 'pen'. Each issue of the serialized form of the novel represents an incomplete unit of narrative text, which remains open to expansion, qualification, or revision in subsequent issues. At the same time, the sketch is a relatively free-standing form, which must possess a sufficiently intrinsic value if it is to maintain the interest of its readers.

Prior to the serialization of *Vanity Fair,* Thackeray wrote numerous fictional and non-fictional 'sketches', often with accompanying visual illustrations, for publication in *Fraser's Magazine, Punch,* and other journals. A volume collection of his early fiction was issued as *Comic Tales and Sketches* in 1841, whilst a number of early magazine articles on artistic, literary, and political affairs in France were published together under the title of *The Paris Sketch Book in* 1840 – a nomenclature that was later repeated with *The Irish Sketch Book* (1843), a more connected narrative account of his tour of Ireland in 1842. Clearly, the connotations of the term 'sketch' vary across the range of such diverse texts. In the case of Thackeray's fiction, it often describes a roughly delineated anecdote or character type, such as the physiognomical sketches of artists, authors, and gamblers that he contributed to Douglas Jerrold's satirical anthology *Heads of the People* (1840–1).[4] The term has a more explicitly visual signification in the case of *The Paris Sketch Book,* which provides a verbal and visual record of Thackeray's residence as an art student in Paris during the late 1830s, whereas in *The Irish Sketch Book* it constitutes a general metaphor for the social observations of journalistic reportage. Although the latter text was, in fact, conceived and published solely in volume form, the genre of the sketch was, in general, tailored to the demands of periodical publication, whether as a self-contained serial, such as *Vanity Fair*, or in the broader context of a magazine. Again, one should point out that Thackeray's use of this genre was by no means unique amongst contemporary writers: Dickens's first book publication was, after all, a collection of journalistic texts entitled *Sketches by Boz* (1836). With Thackeray, however, one could make a case for arguing that the improvisatory and ephemeral character of the sketch was more central to the development of his novelistic aesthetic. This argument has sometimes been used against him, prompting critical debate about whether he was really a 'serious' or 'conscientious' artist, who laboured properly at his craft, or merely a talented journalist whose methods of composition were too improvisatory and haphazard – sketchy in a bad sense.

As Edgar Harden has pointed out, this is a debate that stems originally from Trollope's 1879 critical biography of Thackeray, which, despite lauding him as the greatest novelist of his generation, portrayed him as a 'careless and hasty worker', prone to 'idleness', and artistically compromised by the demands of periodical publication.[5] Significantly, Trollope cited *Henry Esmond* as an exception to these failings, the only one of Thackeray's novels not to be published in serial form. Harden offers a useful defence against such criticism by arguing that Thackeray's serialized fiction 'formalizes incompleteness', rather than being merely form*less*.[6] Yet even in Harden's defence of Thackeray, there is an implicit tendency both to moralize and to naturalize the question of the extent to which his writing inscribes a sufficient quantity of 'labour' or 'industry'. The ironic aspect of this debate is that, on both sides of the argument, it often fails to take into account Thackeray's self-reflexive awareness of the increasing industrialization and commodification of literary production in Victorian society – a point to which I will be returning later in this chapter. The practice of serialization undoubtedly played a crucial role in shaping the narrative and aesthetic form of Thackeray's longer fiction, but this form can be examined with interest in its own right, regardless of the quantity of intentional labour with which its production is invested. Most strikingly, perhaps, his use of the periodical mode of publication produces a peculiar combination of the ephemeral, sketchlike fragment, on the one hand, and a monumental narrative extension, on the other. As Geoffrey Tillotson rightly observed: 'it is probable that no vast work would have come from him at all if the system of publishing in parts, whether separately or in magazines, had not allowed him to write in lengths timed beyond dispute by the public clock.[7] Tillotson's reference to the temporality of serial composition alludes to the fact that, whilst Thackeray was continually forced to write to monthly deadlines, the longer horizon of the completed serial was often measured in years. The immediacy of a journalistic style of writing, focused on the present moment rather than on a distant 'futurity', was thus conjoined with a compulsion to keep on writing over extended periods of time. In 'De Finibus', one of the late *Roundabout Papers*, Thackeray describes his experience of the indeterminate, open-ended nature of serial writing as one that makes *endings* – in literal terms, the inscription of 'finis' – difficult ever fully to attain (*WMT* xii. 369–76).

SIGNATURE AND PARODY

Thackeray's apparent acceptance of the working conditions of the life of the average journalist, as outlined in his essay 'A Brother of the Press', raises questions about his understanding of the nature of authorship that are of particular importance to his writings of the 1830s and 1840s. One of the standard conditions that obtained within journalism of this period was that of anonymous or pseudonymous authorship, and, unlike some of his contemporaries, Thackeray gave public support to this convention. In an article for *Punch* , 'On the Press and the Public' (1850), he argues that 'a newspaper is a composite work got up by many hireling hands' (*WMT* vi. 703), and, thus, acquires a collective identity for which an individualist model of authorship (of the kind designated by Michel Foucault's 'author function'[8]) would be inappropriate. Fittingly, though, the text in which this opinion is voiced is attributed not to

Thackeray himself, but to a 'Dr Solomon Pacifico', one of the many pseudonyms under which his early periodical writings were published. Although the content of 'On the Press and the Public' seems consistent with the views on journalism expressed elsewhere by Thackeray, the very fact of its pseudonymous authorship raises questions about the authenticity of the textual voice: does the article express the real opinions of the biographical individual 'Thackeray', or does 'Dr Solomon Pacifico' speak on behalf of the collective view of *Punch's* 'hireling hands', as was often the case in journals of the period? This is simply a small example of a general problem that confronts the reader of Thackeray's multifarious authorial signatures.

Paradoxically, the invention of recognizable signatures (or authorial personae) was, in all probability, the only way in which a writer in Thackeray's position in the 1830s could begin to establish personal reputation and create commercial opportunities for himself within the periodical market. If the pseudonym functions as a means of concealing the author's 'real' identity from the general public, it nevertheless allows him or her to construct a personalized authorial identity that stands out from the base level of journalistic anonymity. A popular pseudonym could thus be utilized as a form of brand name in order to attract readers, whilst its author's identity would soon become known by editors and fellow writers. At the same time, the use of multiple signatures by the one author would have enabled him or her to maximize income by producing different kinds of texts for different journals, which, if published under the same name, would risk the appearance of inconsistency or of becoming overly familiar to the reader. Thackeray's most frequently used pseudonym was 'Michael Angelo Titmarsh', a figure particularly associated with his essays on literature and visual art for *Fraser's Magazine*, but also credited with the authorship of several early comic tales, the two *Sketch Books* and the popular *Christmas Books* of the late 1840s. In addition, he used the following signatures in periodical publications from 1837 to around 1850: Charles J. Yellowplush, Major Gahagan, Spec, Ikey Solomons, Jr, George Savage FitzBoodle, the Fat Contributor, and the aforementioned Solomon Pacifico. In fact, prior to *Vanity Fair*, virtually none of

Thackeray's texts was published under his own name, and, even after the considerable commercial success of this novel, when most of the signatures listed above lapsed with the discontinuation of his principal periodical affiliations, he continued to practise a form of pseudonymous authorship until the end of his career. Thus, for instance, *The History of Henry Esmond is* a fictitious autobiographical narrative, not only 'written by himself', as is declared on the title page, but also fictitiously 'edited' by his daughter Rachel Esmond Warrington; and, similarly, both *The Newcomes* and *Philip* are narrated by a fictitious writer, the eponymous hero of *Pendennis*. Once again, it might be argued that the cultural context of Thackeray's early journalistic writing plays a germinative role in the development of his later narrative forms and techniques.

Thackeray's obvious penchant for writing under the guise of a fictive persona can, however, be explained in ways other than through the purely pragmatic cultural and economic considerations of periodical publication, as described above. What might have commenced as a merely conventional code of journalistic authorship begins to generate a more intriguing internal logic, which marks his writing in more peculiar ways. Leaving the narrative construction of the later novels for subsequent discussion, one should note, first of all, that Thackeray's early journalistic signatures are not simply abstract grammatical functions, bearing little or no relation to the content of the texts themselves, but are, in many cases, developed into autonomous authorial personalities, each defined by a recognizable and all-pervasive idiolect. Each of these personae, in other words, is endowed with a linguistic reality capable of saturating every aspect of his verbal performances. So, in the case of 'Michael Angelo Titmarsh', for example, one cannot straightforwardly assume that this is the persona that Thackeray adopts in order to express his own views on literature or art, even though this is clearly one function of the signature, because of the way in which Thackeray playfully foregrounds the separate and fallible identity of Titmarsh and his own unique mode of utterance. A more extreme example of the linguistic autonomy of Thackeray's personae, and of its potential for destabilizing the authenticity or truth value of authorial discourse, can be found in *The Memoirs of Mr Charles*

J. Yellowplush. In this series, Thackeray creates the comic idiolect of a snobbish Cockney footman by ventriloquizing a supposed lower-class imitation of 'elevated' and 'respectable' forms of speech, and, thus, simultaneously exposing the dominant class consciousness of fashionable society to satirical laughter. Yellowplush's language generates a rich vein of inventive punning and comic malapropism, at times innocently funny (e.g. 'My tail is droring rabidly to a close') and elsewhere more satirically barbed (e.g. the use of 'Honrabble' as a linguistically disrespectful nod to his superiors) (*WMT* iii. 315). No one, of course, would make the mistake of assuming that Yellowplush speaks directly on behalf of Thackeray in the way that might occur with some of the essays credited to Titmarsh, but the difference between these personae is one of degree, rather than of kind. The more ostensibly fictionalized Yellowplush, for instance, is used to comment directly on 'non-fictional' matters, as we have seen in relation to Thackeray's attack on Bulwer Lytton, while, conversely, an apparently straightforward referential critical discourse attributed to Titmarsh is often interwoven with fanciful discussion of the character of the critic.

One obvious effect of Thackeray's use of multiple signatures, then, is the problem that it creates for any attempt to locate a unified authorial voice for his early writings, encompassing both fictional and non-fictional discourse. The notion of the 'mask' has sometimes been invoked in order to describe his multiplicity of personae, but even this term has the disadvantage of implying the underlying existence of a stable authorial identity, often on the grounds of a supposititious psychology of the need for concealment. An alternative, and in my view more productive, account of the destabilization of authorial identity in Thackeray's writing can be based upon his lifelong fascination with the forms of parody and pastiche. Within the overarching context of journalism, parody is arguably the most characteristic literary form of his early career, and it is, again, one that appears particularly well suited to its original medium of publication. If the periodicals for which Thackeray wrote were, to a large extent, vehicles for literary and political polemic, parody was the form in which he excelled at wounding his victims. Like the medium of the periodical itself, parody can be seen as an inherently intertextual genre that, as Simon Dentith suggests, requires for its effect the reader's recognition of a pre-existing world of texts or other cultural signs.[9] Parody presupposes an awareness of the different, and often antagonistic, forms of literary and cultural discourse, and typically aims to deflate the authority of its chosen target by appearing to speak its own language (through mimicry, in other words). In *The Memoirs of Mr Charles J. Yellowplush*, for instance, Thackeray speaks through the assumed voice of a snobbish Cockney footman so as to parody what he perceives to be a general social phenonemon: the spurious assumption of gentility practised at all levels of an increasingly mobile and unstable class society. Hence, a later incarnation of Yellowplush appears in *Punch* as the newly ennobled C. Jeames de la Plushe, esq. Elsewhere, he produced a number of parodic texts in which the object of mimicry was, quite specifically, the discourse of other authors and of distinct generic forms of writing. The most celebrated example of this more explicitly intertextual form of parody is a series of pastiche fictions entitled *Punch's Prize Novelists* (1847) (or *Novels by Eminent Hands*, in its later volume form) and written in the style of such leading contemporary novelists as Benjamin Disraeli, Charles Lever, G. P. R. James, Fenimore Cooper, Lady Catherine Gore, and Bulwer-Lytton. A later mock-heroic sequel to Walter Scott's *Ivanhoe, Rebecca and Rowena* (1849), can also be included within this body of work. Not all these literary parodies were conceived with a hostile satirical intent, and, indeed, Thackeray characteristically ironizes his own authorial stance by including within *Punch's Prize Novelists* a tale ('Crinoline') attributed to his persona 'Je-mes Pl-sh, Esq.': a self-parody of a parody, it would seem.

There are at least two ways of interpreting the parodic technique of *Punch's Prize Novelists*. On the one hand, and most obviously, it may be read as a vehicle for critique, which seeks to expose the false modes of perception and dangerous moral precepts inscribed within a particular form of fictional discourse by exaggerating this discourse to the point at which its underlying absurdity is revealed. This is the case, for example, with the parodies of Bulwer's hyperbolic Romantic idealism in 'George de Barnwell' and Lever's bloodthirsty tales of military adventure in 'Phil Fogarty: A Tale of the Fighting Onety-Oneth'. But, on the other hand, one is struck, on reading the series, with the possibility that, for Thackeray, all forms of novelistic discourse (and thus, perhaps, all forms of language in general) are susceptible to parodic ventriloquism in equal measure. By including himself – or, rather, one of his many authorial signatures – amongst his list of selected targets, Thackeray undermines the presumption that there exists an unstated normative form of language, capable of standing in judgement over other, more degraded forms. As Dentith has noted, we are left with the impression that his parodic technique relativizes the authority of the parodist himself by reducing language to a multiplicity of competing literary styles.[10] Thus, as in James Joyce's *Ulysses*, parody, in Thackeray, might be said to operate as a principle of citation by which each of the various imitated signatures of language is placed within ironic quotation marks, making it difficult to determine whether there is any linguistic element of the text that is not, in some ways, being quoted. While more of a satire than a parody on the 'silver-fork' novels of Catherine Gore, the final instalment of *Punch's Prize Novelists* ('A Plan for a Prize Novel') may be read as an interpretative key to the series, which comically generalizes the question of stylistic 'branding'. The fictive author of a letter – an 'eminent dramatist' named Brown – outlines a proposal to write a novel that would exist purely for the purpose of advertising brand-name commodities, and, thus, become a self-financing production. Here, one might argue, Thackeray is satirizing the mercenary commercial motivation of the writing of his own series of parodic 'prize novels', but also, perhaps, alluding o the way in which the various literary styles and signatures mimicked within his texts function precisely like brand names, instantly recognizable to the contemporary reader. The impetus behind literary parody and self-parody is derived, ultimately, from the corn-modification of modern literary culture, which makes the invention of authorial personae a profitable business.

The destabilizing linguistic effects of Thackeray's parodic technique cannot be easily reconciled to the serious critical intentions with which several of his parodies were undoubtedly conceived. If there is no untainted normative vantage point from which the parodist writes, the moral purpose that informs his mimicry of other writers' discourse is difficult to sustain. This problem becomes particularly visible in Thackeray's first two novels, both of which are essentially parodic in form and concerned with the issue of the morality of fiction. In *Catherine* he produced a parody of the genre of the 'Newgate novel', a contemporary form of crime fiction popularized by William Harrison Ainsworth (in *Jack Sheppard*), Bulwer-Lytton (Eugene Aram), and Dickens (Oliver Twist), in full awareness that its paradoxical criterion of success would be the abolition of the very form of writing without which it would not exist. In the final chapter of the novel, Thackeray (in the persona of Ikey Solomons, Jr) makes clear what he perceives to have been the guiding moral principle behind his narrative: whereas other Newgate novels incite in their readers a mixture of sympathy and repugnance towards the criminal hero, and a sense of painful pleasure in following his exciting sequence of adventures, this story has sought to produce feelings of unrelieved boredom and disgust. Thus, Solomons serio-comically proclaims a vindication of his work when critics 'abuse the tale of "Catherine" as one of the dullest, most vulgar and immoral works extant', since it was precisely intended to operate as a 'cathartic' medicine, weaning readers off their narcotic addiction to narratives of criminal adventure: 'The public was, in our notion, dosed and poisoned by the prevailing style of literary practice, and it was necessary to administer some medicine that would produce a wholesome nausea, and afterwards bring about a more healthy habit' (*WMT* iv. 669). The problem, however, with this stringently moralistic conception of the function of parody is that it either produces a type of fiction that is unrelentingly negative in effect – one that seeks, ultimately, to argue itself out of existence – or, as Thackeray himself believed of *Catherine*, fails to be 'disgusting enough', and thus ends up generating a surreptitious sympathy for its criminal heroine despite its intention (*LPP* i. 433). Thackeray's first novel exposes in a particularly stark manner the difficulty of combining the linguistically playful aspect of parody with a sober critical message, since the former inevitably feeds off, and perpetuates, the very mode of discourse that the latter is attempting to destroy.

Thackeray's second full-length novel, *The Luck of Barry Lyndon: A Tale of the Last Century* (first serialized in *Fraser's Magazine* in 1844), is also parodic in inspiration, but arguably manages to escape the constricting double-bind that marks the logic of parody in *Catherine*. The most immediate source of intertextual reference in this novel is Charles Lever's *Confessions of Harry Lorrequer* (1839), another popular contemporary fiction, but this time from a somewhat different genre: a romantic autobiography documenting the heroic military exploits of an Irish adventurer. Although, as I have mentioned, Thackeray was suspicious of the romanticization of military life in Lever's fiction, objecting to what he called the 'pugnacious and horse-racious parts of the Lorrequer novels', he was also an affectionate admirer of Lever,[11] and there is no sense in which the aim of *Barry Lyndon is* simply to annihilate the object of its parody. Through its employment of a distinctly unreliable first-person narratorial voice, alongside the additional device of another invented editorial signature, however, the novel maintains Thackeray's preoccupation with the problematic nature of fictional morality and authorial 'truth'.

As in *Catherine*, the central figure of *Barry Lyndon is* a morally questionable character, revealed as a 'rogue' if not a 'criminal' on the evidence of his own words, though we are also made aware of the possibly tenuous nature of this distinction. The use of the first-person narrative form allows Barry to convict himself, the sustained authorial irony behind the bravado of his 'confessions' replacing obtrusive didactic commentary, but it also generates a more complex effect by enabling Barry to present himself in the persuasive or sympathetic light feared by Ikey Solomons, Jr. In the original serialized version of the novel, Thackeray framed Barry's account of his life with a series of editorial footnotes and prefatory remarks attributed to George Savage Fitzboodle (another authorial persona) and 'Oliver Yorke' (the fictitious editor of *Fraser's Magazine*), ostensibly in an attempt to contain this potential for a sympathetic reading of the narrative. It is the editorial apparatus that provides the vein of explicit moral judgement that is absent from the main body of the text, and that, one might think, simplifies the novel as a whole. Yet it might also be argued that the insertion of a competing narrative voice, contradicting Barry's autobiographical ac-count, only adds to the ambiguity of the text, rather than reducing it. It is by no means certain that Fitzboodle speaks authoritatively on behalf of Thackeray, and, indeed, on some occasions, he clearly functions as a spokesman for the conventional notion of morality that the novel aims to satirize. At the opening of Part II, for example, Fitzboodle interrupts Barry's narrative to remark that he 'is glad to think that the reader is speedily about to arrive at that period in the history where poetical justice overtakes the daring and selfish hero of the tale' (*BL* 234). Yet this obtrusive censure of a 'hero' whose dubious character is more subtly revealed through his own narrative is itself contradicted by subsequent footnotes that question the stock novelistic implementation of a morality of 'poetical justice'. Barry does, in the end, receive the 'justice' that his unscrupulous pursuit of fortune deserves, but the manner in which his career is terminated is then exposed as an ironic concession to a debased novelistic convention that confuses moral principle with worldly success. As Fitzboodle himself eventually recognizes, the fact that Barry loses his fortune at the end of his narrative is irrelevant to the moral lesson that can be drawn from it. What the story *has* demonstrated, he contradictorily insists, is that 'worldly success is by no means the consequence of virtue; that if it is effected by honesty sometimes, it is attained by selfishness and roguery still oftener; and that our anger at seeing rascals prosper and good men frequently unlucky, is founded on a gross and unreasonable idea of what good fortune really is' (*BL* 278). The allocation of 'good [or bad] fortune', in other words, does not correspond to the workings of a Divinely ordained moral order, but is essentially a matter of chance. Here, Fitzboodle's interpretation of the narrative carries weight, as the original title *The Luck of Barry Lyndon* (the novel was retitled *The Memoirs of Barry Lyndon* in 1856) corroborates.

In his concluding remarks on Barry's story, Fitzboodle draws together his views on the morality of fiction in a manner reminiscent of Ikey Solomons, Jr., at the end of *Catherine*. The true ethical value of the novel, he argues, resides not in a sentimental desire to administer a form of 'poetical justice' that has no corresponding existence in social reality, but, rather, by returning to the 'old style of Molière and Fielding', in attempting to 'copy nature', and 'hence in describing not only what is beautiful, but what is ill-favoured too, faithfully, so that each may appear as like as possible to nature' (*BL* 310). There can be little doubt that Fitzboodle here expresses a crucial tenet of Thackeray's own literary aesthetic: namely, the moral basis of his consistent defence of realism and equally consistent critique of illusory or idealized forms of art (an issue to which I return in Chapter 3). However, unlike in *Catherine*, the remarks of Thackeray's authorial persona must still be treated with some caution by the reader. For if the underlying message of *Barry Lyndon is* the proposition that novelists must 'copy nature', representing 'truth' in all its forms, however unsavoury, we are left with the unsettling paradox of having read a novel that claims to provide a truthful representation of the story of a liar! Much of the comedy of Barry's narrative derives from the disjunction that exists between the patently exaggerated nature of his self-perception – as, for example, 'one of the most accomplished, the tallest, the most athletic, and the handsomest gentlemen of Europe' (*BL* 178) – and his repeated asseverations of the absolute truthfulness of his claims. Barry's 'truthful' account of his life is clearly meant to be received with the scepticism and, at times, incredulity reserved for a 'tall story' – a type of fabulous storytelling that Thackeray associates (stereotypically enough) with the Irish literary culture from which Barry is drawn. In the narratorial figure of Barry Lyndon, in other words, Thackeray seems to present the very antithesis of the realist writer of fiction endorsed by Fitzboodle, or perhaps a parodic version of that model of the writer – a 'truth-teller' who just cannot be believed. Just as Fitzboodle's editorial comments are designed to undercut Barry's version of events, so one might suggest that Barry's mode of narration subverts the aesthetic and moral principles of his editor. What Barry's story comically reminds us of is the fact that, in an obvious sense, fiction is not meant to be true, and hence, as the Victorian critic Thomas Carlyle concluded, can always be dismissed as a form of lying.[12] – This awareness of the devious and elusive nature of fictional discourse is reinforced by the protean form of Barry's identity as the 'author' of his own life. The name 'Barry Lyndon' is, in fact, only the last of a series of guises adopted by him in the course of his narrative: Redmond Barry, Captain Barry, and Redmond de Balibari are some of his earlier incarnations. Like Thackeray's own multiplicity of authorial personae, then, the proliferation of Barry's signatures further serves to undermine the authenticity of his authorial voice. The egregious fictionality of his identity leads to a dispersal of the sources of truth that rubs against his editor's desire to locate a single ground of meaning in the imitation of nature.

THE (IN)DIGNITY OF LITERATURE

Thackeray once claimed that his parodies of other writers were 'good natured' and 'friendly and meek in spirit', but, unfortunately or not, they were not always received in this spirit (*LPP* ii. 270–1). His skill as a parodist seems to have contributed to the perception, prevalent by the late 1840s, that he held scant respect for the 'dignity' of his own profession, a serious accusation at a time when many writers were consciously seeking to enhance the professional (and thus social) status of authorship. Dickens personally rebuked Thackeray for the 'design' of *Punch's Prize Novelists*, considering it 'a great pity to take advantage of the means our calling gives us with such accursed readiness, of at all depreciating or vulgarizing each other': he had, he assured him, the 'honour and dignity' of the 'literary men' of England at heart (*LPP* ii. 336–7). The criticism of Thackeray as a writer who unceremoniously debunked the pretensions and absurdities of other writers (as well as himself) through satire, parody, and caricature came to a head in the so-called Dignity of Literature controversy that surrounded the publication of *Pendennis* in 1849–50. As Thackeray himself noted in an open letter to the *Morning Chronicle* ('The Dignity of Literature', 1850), he stood accused of 'fostering a baneful prejudice' against the literary profession by 'condescending to caricature . . . literary fellow-labourers' (*WMT* xiii. 629). Understandably, the charge was one that Thackeray was keen to refute, but the basis of his self-defence suggests that his understanding of the true 'dignity of literature' was, indeed, markedly different from that of his critics. *Pendennis* contains his most sustained reflection upon the cultural status and material conditions of the modern literary profession, and the retrospective, semi-autobiographical form of the novel allows it to be viewed as an important document (though not an unmediated factual account) of the development of his early literary and journalistic career.

In the fictional context of *Pendennis* Thackeray continues his debate with Bulwer-Lytton over their conflicting interpretations of the value of modern literary journalism, previously centred upon the life of Laman Blanchard. Like Blanchard, the unheroic 'hero' of the novel, Arthur Pendennis, is a writer whose early Romantic literary aspirations are curtailed on encountering the prosaic reality of the commercial world of journalism and publishing. Thus, Pen's sentimental conception of poetry as a spontaneous expression of unmediated feeling (a simplified late-Romantic interpretation of Wordsworth) is ironically deflated when his first journalistic assignment is to construct a poem to match a pre-designed engraving for one of the annual gift books popular during the early nineteenth century. Pen has previously seen himself as a great Romantic spirit, in the mould of Byron or Goethe's *The Sorrows of Young Werther* (1774), but is now forced, from economic necessity, to adapt his poetic imagination to the pre-existing conditions of material literary production: he must write a poem to illustrate a picture of a 'church porch' and has only a few hours in which to do it. The lesson to be drawn from his initiation into the banal pragmatism of literary hack work is made explicit by Thackeray's narrator. The 'hack' (an abbreviation of 'hackney') is a type of horse at the opposite spectrum from 'Pegasus', the mythological winged horse that conventionally signifies poetic inspiration: but 'when you want to make money by Pegasus (as he must, perhaps, who has no other saleable property), farewell poetry and aerial flights: Pegasus only rises now like Mr Green's balloon, at periods advertised beforehand, and when the spectators' money has been paid' (*P.* 450). The modern 'Pegasus', in other words, is forced to assume the role of the hack, who 'trots in harness, over the stony pavement, and pulls a cart or a cab behind him' (*P.* 450). Unlike Bulwer, however, Thackeray's narrator cautions the reader against feeling excessive pity for the plight of the literary hack: 'I for one am quite ready to protest ... against the doctrine which some poetical sympathizers are inclined to put forward, viz., that men of letters, and what is called genius, are to be exempt from the prose duties of this daily, bread-wanting, tax-paying life, and are not to be made to work and pay like their neighbours' (*P.* 450). If the function of literature has been reduced to the banality of the commodity form, it is only one instance of the general condition of modern culture, and so deserves no special pleading. The writer who 'has no other saleable property' but his capacity to write is in exactly the same position as any other alienated labourer.

This argument, if not the terms of its analysis, is anti-Romantic in the broadest sense, but, more specifically, can be viewed as a critique of the idealized 'hero-worship' of Thomas Carlyle. Whereas Carlyle had heralded the potential of the writer to become a modern figure of the hero in his hugely influential lecture 'The Hero as Man of Letters' (1840),[13] Thackeray systematically dispels the heroic aspirations of the various writers depicted in *Pendennis.* In some respects, the novel is, indeed, an exercise in caricature, as contemporary critics alleged, but, more importantly, it is a caricature that serves the purpose of a *demythologization* of the figure of the author. The effect of worldly experience on Pen's personal development is to strip away the illusions of his Romantic consciousness, and in the sphere of art this requires a disenchantment of the aura of literary 'genius' that belongs to Pen's (and Thackeray's) immediate cultural inheritance. In place of these 'lost ... illusion[s]' (*P.* 345) – the novel is perhaps modelled on the theme of Balzac's earlier *Illusions perdues* (1837–43) – stands a starkly materialist apprehension of the economic function of literary production within the cut-throat world of journalism. Amongst other bohemian writers, the reader is introduced to a reviewer named Bludyer, who, 'after looking through the volumes, would sell them at his accustomed bookstall, and having drunk and dined upon the produce of the sale in a tavern box, would call for ink and paper, and proceed to "smash" the author of his dinner and the novel' (*P.* 454). Here, literature is involved in a brutal logic of commodity exchange, as books are sold for money that buys drink that fuels the production of a review attacking the books on which it feeds, and that is, in turn, exchanged for money. Later on, when Pen writes his first novel, its value as a commodity is made similarly apparent. As Warrington, his cynical confidant, acknowledges, novels can be made literally equivalent to other material products, exchanged for 'silver and gold, and for beef and for liquors, and for tobacco and for raiment' (*P.* 523).

The materialist stance that drives the demythologization of Romantic idealism in *Pendennis is* an element of Thackeray's thought that runs consistently throughout his various reflections on the status of the literary profession. Yet the implications of this stance are, in some ways, difficult to assess. As a satirical exposition of the logic of commodification that effects all aspects of literary and cultural production during the nineteenth century, *Pendennis* might be seen as a text that holds much in common with a Marxist analysis of the fate of art within capitalist society. Unlike Marx, however, Thackeray does not claim to be offering *a critique* of the commodified (literary) labour that his novel clearly identifies: that would require a measure of idealism that he is anxious to rebut. Perversely, it is the apparent indignity of the material constraints of modern literary production that he seizes as the basis for a redefinition of its dignity. The comically prosaic, or 'vulgar', aspects of Pen's experience of the literary world are part of a deeper immersion in a state of corrupt, worldly materiality, out of which there is no easy path of transcendence. Thus, for Thackeray, the true 'dignity of literature' lies in a clear-sighted recognition, and acceptance, of the existing limits of a material reality that other authors of the period may have sought to alleviate, but rarely to change. It is consistent with this attitude that he conceived of literature as essentially a 'trade', rather than a profession, and opposed the attempts of Dickens and Bulwer to create a professional 'Literary Union' during the 1840s. The desire for authors to achieve 'professional' status, but without fundamentally altering the economic imperative of the literary market, serves only to mystify their real social character. Taken to its extreme, this position results in an endorsement of *laissez-faire* political economy that, somewhat implausibly, insists on the meritocratic nature of the market. In 'The Dignity of Literature', for example, Thackeray argues that 'the pen gives a place in the world to men who had none before, a fair place, fairly achieved by their genius, as any other degree of eminence is by any other kind of merit' (*WMT* xiii. 630). The attempt to provide a moral justification for acceptance of the literary market, however, does not conform to the impression created in *Pendennis.* On the contrary, the literary world of the novel is patently an *unfair* place, in which Pen's mediocre talent is sufficient for him to succeed whilst the more deserving Warrington remains in obscurity. Here, Thackeray's worldly representation of the unheroic reality of the modern literary marketplace denies itself the consolation of a residual form of idealism.

The Dignity of Literature controversy would appear to have made a considerable impression on Thackeray's perception of his authorial identity, since he returned to it at almost every available opportunity in his subsequent writings – most explicitly, at the end of his final lecture on 'The English Humourists of the Eighteenth Century' (1852), where he imparts a historical dimension to his previous understanding of the modern literary trade. Whether his position significantly changed as a result of the criticism levelled against *Pendennis*, however, seems doubtful. Right up to the final stages of his career, when he is often supposed to have cultivated the image of bourgeois professional respectability that he had earlier satirized, Thackeray openly declared the monetary incentive behind his writing, making visible the material processes without which his works of literary imagination would not exist. Yet, as I suggest in the following chapter, the workings of the imagination, in Thackeray's fiction, are themselves often material in form.

2

Allegory and the World of Things

VULGAR MATERIALISM

An awareness of the function of literature as a commodity, produced by labour and exchanged with other commodities in order to fulfil material needs and desires, represents one aspect of a much broader strain of materialism within Thackeray's writing. Materialism is by no means an irredeemably negative cultural condition, as far as he is concerned, for it is also equated, on the other hand, with the experience of intense sensory pleasures. In 'On a Lazy Idle Boy' (1860), from *The Roundabout Papers*, for example, Thackeray likened his childhood 'taste' in reading novels to an appetite for eating jelly and other sweets: a form of consumption that is, in both cases, positively defined as infantile, feminine, and oriental (*WMT* xii. 170). According to John Carey, this metaphorical equivalence between literature and food reflects 'a pugnaciously-held belief that the satisfactions of art and of appetite are truly linked, and bring the same parts of the human organism into play'.[1] It is certainly the case that food features prominently within Thackeray's recorded experience of material culture, and that his repeated insistence on the high aesthetic value of fine *cuisine* is only partly facetious. In 'Memorials of Gormandising' (Fraser's Magazine, 1841), Michael Angelo Titmarsh places French cookery alongside music, painting, and architecture as one of the 'polite arts', and, whilst the same aesthetic status is not extended to plain English food, the claim has a more general implication that supports Carey's contention: 'All a man's senses', Titmarsh proclaims, 'are worthy of employment, and should be cultivated as a duty. The senses are the arts' (*WMT* xiii. 576).

The assertion that art is of the same nature as sensory appetite is a deliberately iconoclastic gesture on Thackeray's part, running counter to the philosophical tradition of idealist aesthetics (associated primarily with Immanuel Kant) in which the faculty of 'disinterested' artistic appreciation is firmly distinguished from such 'low' bodily appetites as the desire for food or sex.[2] Thackeray humorously refutes this distinction by juxtaposing, or even conflating, high and low forms of cultural discourse. Thus, in 'A Dinner in the City' (Punch, 1847–8), another example of journalistic food writing, he declares with mock gravity that 'the culinary passages in Scott's novels .. . always were my favourites' (*WMT* vi. 553). The designed effect of such remarks is a teasing vulgarity, consistent with the strategy of demythologizing Romantic 'illusions' about art that was discussed in the preceding chapter. In 'Memorials of Gormandising', Titmarsh makes this ambition dear by moving easily between his recollections of Parisian menus and a comically physiological critique of Byron:

> If you don't like your victuals, pass on to the next article; but remember that every man who has been worth a fig in this world, as poet, painter, *or musician*, has had a good appetite and a good taste. Ah, what a poet Byron would have been had he taken his meals properly, and allowed himself to grow fat – if nature intended him to grow fat – and not have physicked his intellect with wretched opium pills and acrid vinegar, that sent his principles to sleep, and turned his feelings sour! If that man had respected his dinner, he never would have written 'Don Juan'. (*WMT* xiii. 576–7)

The problem with Byron, in other words, was his perverse, artificially suppressed, appetite. Though hardly a demonstrable argument, this contention is a strikingly persistent feature of Thackeray's various satires of Romantic ideology. Denial of the material wants of the body is read as a sign of intellectual pretension or fanaticism that, by concealing the presence of base appetite, allows it to resurface in a more grotesque and monstrous form. Similar examples of this analysis can be found in 'Sorrows of Werther', a poetic parody of Goethe's novel of the same title written in 1851 that refigures Lotte's response to the news of Werther's suicide through the laconic act of buttering some bread, and in the story of 'Ottilia' (1843), from *FitzBoodle's Confessions*, which features an apparently ethereal German woman (bearing the same name as Goethe's sister, whom Thackeray had met during his visit to Weimar in 1830) who, on closer acquaintance, turns out to be an insatiable sausage-eater.

In some respects, then, Thackeray can be seen as one of the most Rabelaisian of Victorian English writers (though this may not be saying much). The demystifying exposure of gross corporeal appetites that marks much of his early journalistic writing places him in the low comic tradition, which stretches from Rabelais to his acknowledged eighteenth-century master, Henry Fielding, and stands in stark contrast to the more sentimental form of humourism practised by Dickens. If Thackeray's attention to the body does not extend as explicitly as that of his predecessors to matters of sexual appetite, the sublimation of sexual desire into the pleasures of eating is often close to the surface, as the story of 'Ottilia' attests. 'Memorials of Gormandising', as Carey notes, reads at times like an extended metaphor for the sexual epicureanism popularly associated with the 'wicked' charm of Paris (*WMT* xiii. 575).[3] The homologous relationship between sensory indulgence in one form and the other is emphasized by Thackeray's defiant response to the moral opprobrium that is attached to both. He refuses to feel any shame at the excessive pleasure that he experiences in eating a beefsteak, and, significantly, denies that such pleasure is effeminate or unmanly. Gormandising, in other words, affords him a somewhat more acceptable channel through which to declare carnal appetites that, in the case of sexual desire, would clearly transgress the normative code of masculine self-restraint. It would be too simplistic, however, to conclude that Thackeray's unabashed insistence on the healthiness of bodily appetites successfully escapes the trammels of 'repressive' Victorian sexual ideology. The gluttonous male body inscribed in the comic dialogue of 'Memorials of Gormandising' may be protected from the tendency to pathologize sensory indulgence, but the same cannot always be said of his representations of female corporeality. Viewed from the perspective of the male narrator, the voracious appetite of Ottilia is evidently disturbing: a comic monstrosity that terminates all thoughts of desire. Conversely, the female body is figured elsewhere in Thackeray's fiction as an object of male desire that is crudely reduced to the metaphorical status of food. In 'The Painter's Bargain', a story published in *The Paris Sketch Book* (1840), the narrator introduces a butcher's daughter named Griskinissa, who is affectionately described by her father as 'as lovely a bit of mutton . . . as ever a man would wish to stick a knife into' (*WMT* v. 58). Though this description may be read as another example of Thackeray's vulgar materialist aspiration to debunk the high-flown idealism that cloaks Victorian representations of natural bodily desire, the misogynistic character of the metaphor is grotesquely de-humanizing, rather than the reverse. The living body of the butcher's daughter is metonymically transformed into dead butcher's meat – food for sexual consumption.

Despite the unashamedly epicurean character of Thackeray's materialism, moreover, it is rare to find an instance in which sensory indulgence does not meet with some form of countervailing check, usually in the form of moral reflection. 'A Dinner in the City', for example, recounts his participation in a sumptuous banquet given by the Lord Mayor of London, describing in detail the menu of turtle soup, duck, and venison, which merges into a 'dizzy mist of gluttony', before abruptly ending on a note of satiated dissatisfaction (*WMT* vi. 559). Thackeray's *Punch* persona 'Spec' is reminded that he has 'had too much', and this recognition of the physiological limits of sensory excess is accompanied by a moral realization of the opposing condition of sensory deprivation (*WMT* vi. 563). The grotesque sight of grease trickling down the faces of the gluttonous guests provokes a moment of salutary revulsion from the feast: 'Who is it that *can* want muffins after such a banquet? Are there no poor? Is there no reason? Is this monstrous belly-worship to exist for ever?' (*WMT* vi. 563). The selfishness and greed exhibited on this occasion are momentarily, and unsanctimoniously, revealed by reference to the poverty of those who have not been invited.

In an essay on Thackeray written in 1944 George Orwell described the 'characteristic flavour' of his early writing as 'the atmosphere of surfeit which belongs to the early nineteenth century, an atmosphere compounded of oysters, brown stout, brandy and water, turtle soup, roast sirloin, haunch of venison, Madeira and cigar smoke'.[4] Material extravagance and excess, he rightly pointed out, saturate the society that is documented in Thackeray's journalism and fiction. But for Orwell, as for John Carey, Thackeray's immersion in the material culture of his age is precisely and simply a form of journalistic documentation, demonstrating 'very little social insight and not even a very clear moral code'.[5] What this reading fails to notice is the acute awareness of the precarious borderline between material 'surfeit' and deprivation that invariably marks his social observations. Hence, Thackeray's representation of material culture (or what Orwell terms his grasp of the 'externals' of social experience) is divided between an extraordinarily precise reproduction of the sensuous particularity of things, on the one hand, and a vision of their radical insubstantiality, on the other. His response to an experience of sensory excess such as the Lord Mayor's banquet is neither one of pure appetitive pleasure nor one of strident moralistic disapproval, but, rather, encompasses both reactions in an unstable compound.

THE SOCIAL MEANING OF THINGS

Following Orwell, almost all modern critics of Thackeray have been struck by the extent to which his writing contains, in the words of Barbara Hardy, 'not only a history, but a sociology and a moral psychology, of the world of objects'. While opinions have differed over the nature of his response to this 'world of objects' – from Hardy's identification of a 'radical disgust' at the spectacle of social excess to Carey's countervailing emphasis on an epicurean immersion in sensory experience – the material density of his texts is not in question.[6] From the beginning of his career, material *things* occupy a crucial place in Thackeray's fiction, not merely as aids to the construction of an empirically observed cultural milieu, but also as functional elements within the construction of narrative plot. Several of his comic tales of the 1840s (pre-*Vanity Fair*) feature objects that are invested with a magical capacity to determine the course of an individual's life, always with disastrous consequences.

'The Fatal Boots' (1840), for example, revolves around the desire of its narrator, Bob Stubbs, to acquire a pair of boots in order to complete his costume as a schoolboy dandy. For all his elegant attire, Bob is 'dissatisfied': 'I wanted *a pair of boots.* Three boys in the school had boots – I was mad to have them too' (*WMT* iii. 549). In this instance, the compelling urge to possess material objects remains strangely abstract; in fact, quite the reverse of the sensuous appetite displayed in 'Memorials of Gormandising'. What matters to the narrator is not the concrete particularity of the boots themselves, but the general system of social meaning into which they can be inserted. The boots come to represent Bob's broader social aspiration, his longing to be a 'gentleman and not a trades-man', and thus take on a synecdochic function within the text (*WMT* iii. 553). Yet, at every turn, his unscrupulous schemes to acquire fortune and status are frustrated, and the consequences of his initial attempt to cheat the German boot-maker Stiffel-kind signify a comic 'fatality' that haunts him to the end. The target of Thackeray's satire, here, is relatively transparent: the misguided pursuit of 'gentility' produces a mean-spirited, avaricious desire for objects (including people) that has little to do with the sensuous enjoyment of material things. Bob is figured as a somewhat inept capitalist, who, from an early age, seeks to manipulate the world of objects in order to achieve maximum profit for himself, but the moral lesson of his story suggests that such efforts constitute a false economy.

A similar narrative, both in terms of the object of its satire and in its use of objects for satire, is 'The History of Samuel Titmarsh and the Great Hoggarty Diamond' (1841), perhaps the most brilliant of Thackeray's early comic tales. Here, the world of things is evoked both through detailed observation of material particulars and through the allegorical significance with which certain objects are charged. The Hoggarty diamond – a family heirloom gifted to the hero of the story – plays a similar role to that of the 'fatal boots' in comically presiding over the events of the narrative, but the magical power ascribed to objects is even further exaggerated in this case. The diamond pin that Sam Titmarsh (a cousin of Michael Angelo) wears proudly in his breast is not only an object that represents, synecdochically, his broader social aspiration, but is also one that appears to bear a direct causal responsibility for determining the course of his life. It is the gift of the diamond that first causes Sam to assume a gentlemanly status, exceeding his economic resources, and that then impresses his shady employer Brough, head of the 'Independent West Diddlesex Fire and Life Insurance Company', thus leading to a ruinous involvement in financial speculation (*WMT* iii. 9). An inanimate object, in other words, is credited with an agency commonly reserved for animate subjects. This erasure of the distinction between human and non-human attributes closely resembles what Marx, writing somewhat later in the nineteenth century, was to define as the 'fetishism' attached to the commodity form.[7] Sam's bemused apprehension of the talismanic power of the Great Hoggarty Diamond is, indeed, fetishistic in the Marxian sense, endowing the commodity – a product of social labour – with both human and divine qualities. Thackeray's representation of such fetishism ironizes a society in which the persuasive simulation of wealth and social status proves, temporarily at least, more effective than the tangible possession of economic resources. The diamond, it transpires, is more lucrative for its owner than an equivalent value in money by giving him access to an economy based on credit (or, literally, credibility) that functions through the display of conspicuous signs of social prestige.

Appearance is important to Sam: like the narrator of 'The Fatal Boots' he is one of Thackeray's cut-price dandies, whose 'look' is assembled from carefully selected commodities, though in this text the cultural signification of the object world is rendered with greater specificity. On the day of his chance encounter with an Irish Countess in chapter 3, for instance, Sam recalls wearing 'my blue coat and brass buttons, nankeen trousers, a white sprig waistcoat, and one of Dando's silk hats, that had just come in in the year '22, and looked a great deal more glossy than the best beaver' (*WMT* iii. 19). This is one of innumerable examples in Thackeray's fiction where the commodified status of material culture is precisely, but unobtrusively, articulated. Sam's reference to 'Dando's silk hats' designates the name of the shop from which the article has been purchased as an inseparable aspect of its identity. The hat is branded into the form of a monopoly commodity, and, like any current allusion to Nike or Levis, the act of brand naming is tacitly assumed to be significant: to reveal something of the social identity to which its wearer either adheres or aspires. This revelatory semiotic function of the commodity form is illustrated a few lines later when the Countess points to Sam's friend Gus as 'that ojous vulgar wretch, with the iron heels to his boots, and the big mouth, and the imitation goold neck-chain, who *steered* at us so as we got into the carr'age' (*WMT* iii. 19). Gus, in fact, belongs to the same social group as Sam – both are lowly clerks – but, lacking the aid of the diamond presumably, his choice of jewelry gives him away. The 'imitation goold' of his neck-chain presents an illusion of status that is easily seen through. Viewed from a different perspective, however, the Hoggarty diamond is itself an embodiment of the capacity for illusion inscribed within all commodities; the magical power with which it is invested may be read as a comic allegorization of the phenomenon of commodity fetishism in general. In this respect, the fantastic elements of the story coincide precisely with its realistic documentation of contemporary material culture.

As Carey points out, Thackeray's fiction shows little interest in the processes by which commodities are manufactured, except (as we have seen) in the case of literature itself.[8] The genre of the 'industrial novel', developed contemporaneously by Gaskell and Dickens in the 1840s and 1850s, is entirely foreign to his cultural experience. Yet, as an observer of the spectacle of commodity consumption, Thackeray is arguably unrivalled among novelists of the early-to-mid-Victorian period. Shops – and, more specifically, shop windows – are important signifying spaces, which appear recurrently throughout his early fiction. It is within the medium of the shop window that the illusory capacity of the commodity (its mode of appearance) becomes central to the construction of its social meaning, and this is also where the question of how the commodity has been produced tends to disappear from view. A particularly interesting illustration of this process can be found in 'A Little Dinner at Timmins's' (1848), my final example of Thackeray's tales of misplaced social aspiration.

Fitzroy Timmins is a genteel inhabitant of 'Lilliput Street', living in comparatively straitened circumstances, whose frustrated exclusion from the 'Brobdingnagian' world of elevated social status is symbolized by his longing gaze through the windows of Fubsby's 'magnificent' confectionary shop (*WMT* vi. 707, 721). This shop displays not only 'the most wonderful and delicious cakes and confections in the window, but at the counter there are almost sure to be three or four of the prettiest women in the whole of this world, with little darling caps of the last French make, with beautiful wavy hair, and the neatest possible waists and aprons' (*WMT* vi. 721). Not surprisingly, Fitz (with the collusion of the narrator) proceeds to conflate these two objects of desire, transposing the alluring quality of the commodities onto their human cohabitants:

> Yes, there they sit; and others, perhaps, besides Fitz have cast a sheep's eye through those enormous plate-glass window-panes. I suppose it is the fact of perpetually living among such a quantity of good things that makes those young ladies so beautiful. They come into the place, let us say, like ordinary people, and gradually grow handsomer and handsomer, until they grow out into the perfect angels you see. It can't be otherwise: if you and I, my dear fellow, were to have a course of that place, we should become beautiful too. They live in an atmosphere of the most delicious pine-apples, blanc-manges, creams (some whipt, and some so good that of course they don't want whipping), jellies, tipsy-cakes, cherry-brandy – one hundred thousand sweet and lovely things. (*WMT* vi. 721)

Here, one might argue, the metonymy of women and food performs the same reifying gesture as we saw in the case of Griskinissa, the butcher's daughter, though the materials with which the substitution is made might be thought more appropriately 'feminine'. The narrator's self-conscious awareness of the blurring of persons and things, however, suggests a somewhat more complex analysis of the relationship between commodity fetishism and sexual desire. Humans are thought to take on the characteristics of the commodities with which they are contiguous: hence, the social aspiration that drives the desire to consume commodities can also be expressed in terms of erotic longing and fulfilment. From the perspective of the aspirational Fitz, Fubsby's confectionary shop is a veritable

'Garden of Eden', a paradisical world that promises to fulfil all his desires – social, sexual, and appetitive (*WMT* vi. 722). Thackeray, however, takes pains to disabuse Fitz of this fantasy by taking him behind the scenes of the illusory shop window in a characteristic moment of disenchantment. When Fitz returns to the shop a week after his initial visit, he discovers the shop assistants 'drinking tea out of blue cups, and eating stale bread-and-butter, when his absurd passion instantly vanished' (*WMT* vi. 723).

In each of these three early tales, then, the consumption of commodities is linked to an acute consciousness of the stratification of class society, and of the mechanisms by which cultural 'distinction' (in the sense defined by the sociologist Pierre Bourdieu) is recognized and confirmed. The social meanings attached to the commodity make it as much an abstract cultural sign as a concrete material object. This abstraction is expressed in the form of these tales, which is that of a moral fable or comic allegory, rather than a purely realistic narrative. What the nature of Thackeray's moral position is, however, must now be considered. On one level, the failure of social aspiration in each of the stories would seem to inscribe a politically conservative satire on the folly of seeking to escape one's inherited class position. Despite individual differences of character, the error committed by Bob Stubbs, Samuel Titmarsh, and Fitzroy Timmins is essentially the same: that of aspiring to an elevated, gentlemanly status, that is both beyond their economic means and outside their sphere of cultural competence. The comic treatment of their deluded ambition might, thus, seem to be a way of policing existing boundaries of social class out of a primarily defensive impulse. Viewed in this light, commodities play a decidedly subversive role in the narratives, since it is their capacity for manufacturing illusions which is seen to facilitate, and incite, the transgression of inherited social distinctions. Acquisition of the right kind of commodity allows someone of a low social status to simulate a class identity that is not 'naturally' theirs.

This is an anxiety that resonates obsessively throughout Thackeray's fiction, and is often dramatized through the agonistic relationship between masters and their servants. In *Vanity Fair*, for example, we witness Joseph Sedley's Belgian servant Isidor coveting his master's goods in a famous episode set on the eve of the battle of Waterloo:

> As he helped Jos through his toilsome and complicated daily toilette, this faithful servant would calculate what he should do with the very articles with which he was decorating his master's person. He would make a present of the silver essence-bottles and toilette knicknacks to a young lady of whom he was fond; and keep the English cutlery and the large ruby pin for himself. It would look very smart upon one of the fine frilled shirts, which, with the gold-laced cap and the frogged frock coat, that might easily be cut down to suit his shape, and the captain's gold-headed cane, and the great double ring with the rubies, which he would have made into a pair of beautiful ear-rings, he calculated would make a perfect Adonis of himself, and render Mademoiselle Reine an easy prey . . . So while Monsieur Isidor with bodily fingers was holding on to his master's nose, and shaving the lower part of Jos's face, his imagination was rambling along the Green Avenue, dressed out in a frogged coat and lace, and in company with Mademoiselle Reine; he was loitering in spirit on the banks, and examining the barges sailing slowly under the cool shadows of the trees by the canal, or refreshing himself with a mug of Faro at the bench of a beer-house on the road to Laeken. (*VF* 375)

The aspirational desire of the consumer is linked, here, to the disturbing possibility of a violent reversal of existing class relations. One small slip of the razor and Isidor would gain possession of Jos's luxurious accessories. Not only that, the servant could then take the place of his master, putting on his stolen clothes and successfully impersonating the indolent lifestyle of a gentleman. The fact that Isidor expresses an allegiance to the cause of Napoleon gives a further ironic indication as to the 'revolutionary' effects of the commodity form on traditional social hierarchies. As with the more central figure of Becky Sharp, Isidor's projected upward mobility through society can be deemed meritocratic in the sense that the ability to acquire and display commodities, by whatever means necessary, is not dependent upon the hereditary principle. It would be a mistake, however, to conclude from this that Thackeray's anxiety over the destabilizing tendency of the commodity places him entirely on the side of the an*cien régime.*

THE SNOBS OF ENGLAND

In fact, Thackeray's most notable contribution to the discourse of social class in Britain was his virtually single-handed codification and critique of the figure of the 'snob'. An understanding of his use of this term is of central importance to any discussion of class consciousness within his fiction. In his *Punch* serial *The Snobs of England. By One of Themselves* (1846–7) (later republished as *The Book of Snobs*), Thackeray not only achieved his first significant popular success as a writer, but also set out a blueprint for the satirical analysis of Victorian class society, which sheds light on both his subsequent and his preceding works. The modern definition of the word 'snob' was, to a large extent, popularized by Thackeray's writings, yet it does not do justice to the rich semantic ambiguity of the term as inherited and developed by him. Whereas a snob is now uniformly defined as 'one who despises those who are considered inferior in rank, attainment,, or taste' (OED), the definition more commonly used by Thackeray is its antithesis: 'one who meanly or vulgarly admires and seeks to imitate, or associate with, those of superior rank or wealth; one who wishes to be regarded as a person of social importance' (OED). The sketches that comprise *The Snobs of England* are, for the most part, illustrations of varying manifestations of the type of social emulation and conspicuous consumption that we have seen in 'The Fatal Boots' and 'The History of Samuel Titmarsh and the Great Hoggarty Diamond'. Thackeray makes it clear that the snob's vulgar attempt to imitate his social superiors does not represent an aspiration to attain what is genuinely worthy of respect or envy, but, rather, a 'mean' admiration of 'mean things' (*WMT* vi. 311). Snobbishness is, in this sense, equivalent to idolatry: a worship of false gods, which runs directly counter to the ideal of 'hero-worship' espoused by Carlyle. Yet the ambiguity of the concept derives from its designation of both those who are 'snobbishly mean' in worshipping their supposed social superiors and those who are 'snobbishly arrogant' in receiving the worship of their supposed inferiors (*WMT* vi. 314). Moreover, these two antithetical forms of snobbishness are conceived as different sides of the same coin: the aspiration of the 'mean' snob is to become an 'arrogant' snob, who looks down on those below him, but in so doing the 'arrogant' snob reveals his own 'meanness', which can be interpreted as an anxious response to the instability of class boundaries.

It is Thackeray's discovery of the underlying identity of these apparently opposing characteristics of the snob that motivates the explicitly self-reflexive character of his satire. Writing *The Snobs of England* as a self-confessed snob allows him to acknowledge the shifting nature of the term as it comes under reflection. Thus, almost the first example of snobbishness that the text provides – that of a man who eats peas with his knife – is itself strangely snobbish for a modern reader. Thackeray later concedes this point, recognizing that his own preliminary definition of the snob, as a vulgar social aspirant who wears the wrong kind of boots or gloves, is more snobbish than the traits to which he had previously affixed the label. If, at times, he appears to exploit the elasticity of this label for the sake of expedience, it is also essential for establishing his broader satirical point that England is 'Snobland' (*WMT* vi. 413). Caught between the antagonistic polarities of aristocratic class distinction and bourgeois commodity culture, 'it is impossible, in our condition of society, not to be sometimes a Snob' (*WMT* vi. 314), he concludes. This acknowledgement of complicity in the condition of snobbishness, however, does not prevent Thackeray's satire from ranging beyond a characteristically indulgent, self-mocking 'tone of playfulness and sentiment' into 'savage' invective (*WMT* vi. 413). Indeed, *The Snobs of England* contains some of the most radical and impassioned social criticism that Thackeray ever wrote. In his 'Concluding Observations on Snobs', for example, he writes with a moral sincerity worthy of the prophetic voice of Carlyle himself:

> I can bear it no longer – this diabolical invention of gentility which kills natural kindliness and honest friendship. Proper pride, indeed! Rank and precedence, forsooth! The table of ranks and degrees is a lie, and should be flung into the fire. Organise rank and precedence! that was well for the masters of ceremonies of former ages. Come forward, some great marshal, and organise Equality in society, and your rod shall swallow up all the juggling old Court gold-sticks. If this is not gospel-truth – if the world does not tend to this – if hereditary-great-man worship is not a humbug

> and an idolatry – let us have the Stuarts back again, and crop the Free Press's *ears* in the pillory. (*WMT* vi. 462)

Here, the aristocratic principle of hereditary class distinction is rebuked as an outmoded superstition that will dissolve under the counter-spell of social 'Equality' – a classic gesture of enlightenment rationality. But, in the same breath, Thackeray attacks the 'mammoniacal superstition' (echoing Carlyle's 'Gospel of Mammonism'[9]), the bourgeois principle that colludes in the veneration of established wealth (*WMT* vi. 462). Each contributes to the formation of a society of snobs, in which unnatural and dishonest relations between the classes are enshrined.

This is not to say that Thackeray's vision of a snob-free world entails the abolition of class society as such. In a letter to his mother, written in the revolutionary year of 1848, the limitations of Thackeray's social radicalism are clearly revealed. While expressing some measure of support for the 'social republic' recently established in France, he rejects 'communism socialism or Louis Blanc' as viable solutions to the conflict between 'property and labour'. The poverty that he acknowledges to be a consequence of the capitalist organization of industrial labour is viewed as an irresolvable problem – a 'mystery' that requires 'something almost equal to a Divine Person to settle'. Hence, social inequality between worker and capitalist is conceived as an immutable condition; morally regrettable, but a necessary evil, akin to 'death disease winter or any other natural phenomenon' (*LPP* ii. 355–7). In this light, the radical stance of *The Snobs of England* might, perhaps, be characterized as a form of bourgeois social republicanism, which seeks to purify the 'natural' laws of capitalism from the artificial accretions of cultural status that surround them, whilst adding in their place a received Christian suspicion of the accumulation of wealth. It is interesting to note that one of the later issues of *The Snobs of England* contains a reference to 'Vanity Fair', the biblical metaphor for a corrupt, worldly society, dedicated to the worship of Mammon, which Thackeray was simultaneously beginning to explore in his next serial (*WMT* vi. 440).

VANITY FAIR

Vanity Fair is Thackeray's most sustained and self-conscious allegorical representation of a society that has become reduced to a world of things. The term 'Vanity Fair' is itself invested with allegorical meaning in Thackeray's imagination: it comes to personify an entire socio-historical condition that, in its own way, is equivalent to the 'Condition of England' explored, more directly, by other novelists of the 1840s. It has a life beyond the text in which it is most famously inscribed, recurring habitually in almost all Thackeray's subsequent novels. Beyond its biblical origins, the most important source for this term is John Bunyan's popular Protestant allegory *The Pilgrim's Progress* (1678), in which Vanity is the name of a town at which a Fair is held that 'last[s] all the year long'. Bunyan's Vanity Fair is a place which represents the dangerous allure of all worldly pleasures that confront the Christian pilgrim on his journey to the Celestial City: 'at *this Fair* are all such Merchandize sold, as Houses, Lands, Trades, Places, Honours, Preferments, Titles, Countreys, Kingdoms, Lusts, Pleasures, and Delights of all sorts, as Whores, Bauds, Wives, Husbands, Children, Masters, Servants, Lives, Blood, Bodies, Souls, Silver, Gold, Pearls, Precious Stones, and what not'.[10] Thackeray's text adopts not merely the name of Bunyan's place of worldly corruption, but also, in parodic form, the allegorical inventory of its contents. In the first paragraph of 'Before the Curtain' (a preface to the main narrative written for its subsequent volume publication), the 'Manager of the Performance' enumerates the merchandise that his Fair has to offer:

> There is a great quantity of eating and drinking, making love and jilting, laughing and the contrary, smoking, cheating, fighting, dancing, and fiddling: there are bullies pushing about, bucks ogling the women, knaves picking pockets, policemen on the look-out, quacks (*other* quacks, plague take them!) bawling in front of their booths, and yokels looking up at the tinselled dancers and poor old rouged tumblers, while the light-fingered folk are operating upon their pockets behind. Yes, this is VANITY FAIR; not a moral place certainly; nor a merry one, though very noisy. (*VF* 1)

Unlike Bunyan, however, Thackeray's narratorial persona is immediately implicated in the world of moral corruption which he exhibits before the reader. 'Vanity Fair' is both the name of the place into which the narrator conducts us and, of course, the title of the novel in which this exhibition is contained. As the 'Manager of the Performance', the narrator draws attention to his role in staging this dubious moral spectacle, and thus leaves himself open to the charge of profiteering from it. Thackeray tacitly disavows the transcendent moral perspective implied within Bunyan's allegory, reducing the status of his persona to that of a 'quack' amongst 'other quacks'.

The rhetoric of Christian allegorical tradition is pervasive throughout *Vanity Fair,* but one of the most immediate problems facing the reader, then, is that of interpreting its uncertain and shifting moral foundation. In 1847, again writing to his mother, Thackeray described the aim of the novel as to show 'a set of people living without God in the world (only that is a cant phrase) greedy pompous mean perfectly self-satisfied for the most part and at ease about their superior virtue' (*LPP* ii. 309). So while he evidently took seriously the prevailing contemporary understanding of the moral responsibility of the novelist, declaring in the same year that the writer's vocation was as important as that of the 'Parson' (*LPP* ii. 282), he was also acutely aware of the inadequacy of espousing conventional pieties: the 'cant phrase' or 'self-satisfied' assumption of 'superior virtue'. In his later novel *Philip,* the inherent fallibility of the novelist-as-moral teacher is expressed in the syllogism: 'All is vanity, look you: and so the preacher is vanity, too' (*WMT* xi. 271). Likewise, in *Vanity Fair,* the sententious role of the preacher is simultaneously affirmed and undermined: the moral purchase that it provides on a Godless world is both necessary to the critical purpose of the novel and yet incapable of escaping the force of its critique.

In his influential study of seventeenth-century baroque allegory, *The Origin of German Tragic Drama* (1925), Walter Benjamin observed a stark contrast between the timeless uniformity of the emblematic inscription, 'vanitas vanitatum vanitas', and the transient nature of the allegorical texts themselves. This contradiction is ironically appropriate because, within the Christian tradition, Benjamin points out, 'an appreciation of the transience of things, and the concern to rescue them for eternity, is one of the strongest impulses in allegory'.[11] A similar contradiction between the assertion of moral transcendence and the acknowledgement of worldly transience is at work within Thackeray's ironic allegory. The allegorical framework of the narrative – commencing with 'Before the Curtain' and ending in the paragraph which begins with the exclamation 'Ah! *Vanitas Vanitatum!* Which of us is happy in this world?' (*VF* 878) – can be viewed as a strategy that seeks to redeem the transient nineteenth-century world of fashionable society by fixing it within the context of an 'eternal' myth: that of the universal failure of human desires. Yet, since Thackeray is conscious of writing from a position within 'Vanity Fair', he is forced to recognize the potentially transient nature of his own text. As a novel that parodies the genre of the 'fashionable novel', popularized by the likes of Disraeli and Bulwer-Lytton in the 1820s and 1830s, *Vanity Fair is* doubly defined by the ephemerality of social and literary fashion. The narrator confesses as much when he remarks, in passing, that 'the best ink for Vanity Fair use would be one that faded utterly in a couple of days' (*VF* 230): the joke being that in the world of fashionable society, as in the writing of fashionable novels or their parodies, nothing is really indelible.

Another characteristic of the baroque Christian allegories discussed by Benjamin, which is of importance to *Vanity Fair,* is the melancholic nature of their contemplation of the transience of worldly desires. At the very beginning of 'Before the Curtain', 'as the Manager of the Performance . . . looks into the Fair, a feeling of profound melancholy comes over him in his survey of the bustling place' (*VF* 1). Later on, in chapter XIX, the narrator expresses a desire to share his sense of melancholy with the reader: 'This, dear friends and companions, is my amiable object – to walk with you through the Fair, to examine the shops and the shows there; and that we should all come home after the flare, and the noise, and the gaiety, and be perfectly miserable in private' (*VF* 228). If *Vanity Fair* may be described as a comic novel, akin to some of the stories that I discussed earlier, its tone is clearly not one of unrelieved hilarity. Significantly, the comedic persona that is represented in Thackeray's illustrations to the novel conforms closely to the archetypal figure of the sad clown. One explanation of this emphasis upon the melancholy experience of 'Vanity Fair' can again be found in terms of Thackeray's critical response to a culture saturated by the exhibition of commodities. Whereas in 'A Little Dinner at Timmins's' the window display of Fubsby's confectionary shop is mediated, primarily, through the enchanted eyes of Fitzroy Timmins, the narrator of *Vanity Fair* observes its 'shops and . .. shows' with a perfectly disenchanted gaze. This response befits the temperament of the (ironic) Christian allegorist whose melancholy derives from a capacity to see through the sensuous and transient allure of worldly things, viewing in its place only the dead matter, or mortified flesh, which, from the perspective of eternity, all material objects are destined to become.

As Andrew Miller has recently observed, objects are routinely associated with death, or with surrogate forms of loss, in *Vanity Fair*.[12] Symbolically, the most striking example of this analogy occurs during the scene in chapter LIII, when Rawdon Crawley discovers Becky's compromising liaison with Lord Steyne. In this narratively climactic moment, Becky is clearly identified with the material possessions that she has acquired through her adulterous relationship with Steyne, to the point of embodying her objectified status as a 'bought' woman:

> The wretched woman was in a brilliant full toilette, her arms and all her fingers sparkling with bracelets and rings; and the brilliants on her breast which Steyne had given her . . . She clung hold of his coat, of his hands; her own were all covered with serpents, and rings, and baubles . . . The drawers were all opened and their contents scattered about, – dresses and feathers, scarfs and trinkets, a heap of tumbled vanities lying in a wreck. (*VF* 675–7)

The scene emblematizes the depth of Becky's moral and sexual corruption in the 'heap of tumbled vanities' that surrounds her. In allegorical terms, this collection of frivolous objects carries the same revelatory force as the 'death's head' in a baroque painting or play. It reminds us not only of the fact that the possession of material things is an inherently precarious business, given that property is always alienable from its owner, but also that the possessor of things is herself a material (and hence mortal) body. This revelation is sustained by the following chapter (LIV) in which we witness the dismantling of Becky's domestic establishment, as servants and creditors discover the breakdown of her marital relationship with Rawdon, and make off with her possessions in lieu of payment. Yet the dissolution of Becky's 'heap of tumbled vanities' is merely one example of the universal fate of ownership in *Vanity Fair*. Objects are laboriously accumulated during life only to be auctioned off, or repossessed, upon death or financial ruin. John Sedley's bankruptcy, for instance, leads to a public auction of his property in chapter XVII, at which his rival Mr Osborne acquires some 'famous port wine' (*VF* 205). The futility of Osborne's triumph, though, is revealed when his own death is similarly couched in terms of material dispossession: his 'house was dismantled; the rich furniture and effects, the awful chandeliers and dreary blank mirrors packed away and hidden' (*VF* 779). Death, indeed, becomes equivalent to the condition of bankruptcy in the world of 'Vanity Fair', and vice versa. The scene of Sedley's auction reminds the narrator of the 'obsequies of a departed friend' (*VF* 200). Without possessions, that is to say, the inhabitants of the Fair may as well be dead, an inference that can be drawn, conversely, from the way in which death itself is represented as a form of financial ruin.

If Thackeray's baroque allegorical treatment of the mortification of worldly things frames the narrative of *Vanity Fair* within an apparently timeless context of frustrated human desire, its more specific historical character is also recognizable. The conspicuous and unceasing circulation of objects within the world of the text offers a microcosm of the circulation of commodities within the industrial capitalist society in which it was produced (as a commodity). The fact that *Vanity Fair* was published in the same year as Marx and Engels's *Communist Manifesto (1848)* is not a mere historical coincidence, for, in many respects, they share a similar understanding of the restless, cyclical energy of modern capitalism. Where *The Communist Manifesto* fashions an image of a society in which 'all fixed, fast-frozen relations, with their train of ancient and venerable prejudices and opinions, are swept away, all new-formed ones become antiquated before they can ossify . . . [a]ll that is solid melts into air',[13] Thackeray provides a congruent fictional exposition of the paradoxical insubstantiality of the world of things. Likewise, Thackeray's narrative replicates the instability of economic fortunes under capitalism, as it pursues the rise and fall of its characters through the ranks of fashionable 'society'. While Sedley and Osborne are official representatives of mercantile speculation, whose contrasting fortunes embody the risks and rewards that it incurs, Becky Sharp is also a notable speculator (as her surname suggests) who operates within the unofficial sphere of private society – the only market that is accessible to her as a woman. Less obtrusively, Thackeray reveals how the individual narratives of all his characters are shaped by their dependence upon an impersonal economic system. For instance, Amelia Sedley, initially a victim of her father's ill-fortune, is equally dependent upon 'good fortune' in returning to the 'genteel world' later in the novel (*VF* 761). This is demonstrated when her brother Jos returns from India to set up a domestic establishment in London:

> he engaged a comfortable house of a second-or third-rate order in Gillespie Street, purchasing the carpets, costly mirrors and handsome and appropriate planned furniture by Seddons, from the assignees of Mr Scape, lately admitted partner into the great Calcutta house of Fogle, Fake, and Cracksman, in which poor Scape had embarked seventy thousand pounds, the earnings of a long and honourable life, taking Fake's place, who retired to a princely park in Sussex (the Fogies have been long out of the flint, and Sir Horace Fogle is about to be raised to the peerage as Baron Bandanna) – admitted, I say, partner into the great agency house of Fogle and Fake two years before it failed for a million, and plunged half the Indian public into misery and ruin . . . To be brief, Jos stepped in and bought their carpets and sideboards, and admired himself in the mirrors which had reflected their kind handsome faces. (*VF* 761–2)

Characteristically, Thackeray emphasizes, here, that Jos's good fortune in acquiring furniture for his new home derives from someone else's ruin. As Amelia consequently rises in society, so the previously unmentioned figure of 'poor Scape' falls. In *Vanity Fair* the accumulation of material wealth is never devoid of costs. Profit and loss are inseparably interwoven within a potentially interminable cycle of narrative events. The indifference of objects to their transitory owners generates both the irony and the pathos of this vision. Jos, complacently admiring himself in the mirror that has just as happily reflected the 'handsome faces' of its previous owners, presents a brilliant emblem of the 'vanity' (in both senses of the word) that underpins the reflected glory of material possession.

The insertion of this miniature narrative, detailing the financial failure of the 'great Calcutta house of Fogle, Fake, and Cracksman', is also significant for its suggestion of the geographical extension of the economic system that determines the fortune of individual characters. Thackeray's fictional world of things is genuinely a global market, reflecting an awareness of the intimate association between commercial and imperial expansion – another point of similarity to *The Communist Manifesto. His* apprehension of the economic gains and risks of empire was, no doubt, informed by personal experience: born in Calcutta to a family with extensive connections to the East India Company, Thackeray lost his private fortune largely as a result of ruinous financial speculation on the subcontinent. In *Vanity Fair*, India is represented as a site both of selfless military service, to which Dobbin is exiled after seeing action at Waterloo, and of voracious commodity consumption, epitomized by the corpulent figure of Jos Sedley. It is Jos's 'honourable and lucrative post' as the '[ex-]collector of Boggley Wollah' (*VF* 27), however, that proves more integral to the novel's ironic perspective: just as Jos's function is to collect taxation revenue from his Indian subjects, so, in turn, his dubiously acquired wealth becomes a collectable item for Becky Sharp. The acquisitions of empire, thus, feed directly into the domestic marriage market. Indeed, according to Gary Dyer, the term 'Vanity Fair' is itself redolent of the Oriental bazaar: an arena of commercial exchange that was figured as synonymous with sexual corruption during the nineteenth century.[14] In this light, Becky's disreputable association with 'booths', 'bazaars', and 'Fancy Fairs' bears interrelated connotations of both sexual commodification (or prostitution) and oriental otherness.

A similar analogy can be drawn between the commercial spectacle displayed within *Vanity Fair* and that of the 'Great Exhibition', which opened at London's Crystal Palace in 1851. The Great Exhibition was the first of many similar events staged during the latter half of the nineteenth century that were designed to display and celebrate the material achievements of industrial society in the form of commodities assembled from around the world. Precursors to the modern trade fair, these exhibitions were testimony to the emergence of a global capitalist market, controlled from the main centres of European imperialism. What is often considered significant about the structure of the Crystal Palace, moreover, is its framing of the contents of the Exhibition through a medium composed primarily of glass. As Miller has argued, the Great Exhibition marks the construction of a new cultural and epistemological space for the representation of the commodity form, which bears more than a passing resemblance to the textual space constructed three years earlier in *Vanity Fair*.[15] Thackeray's 'Manager of the Performance', as we have seen, models the exhibition of his fictive world upon the image of the commercial shop-window display, although, unlike the Great Exhibition, which was designed to promote the desirability of the commodity, the spectacle is one that provokes in him a mood of melancholic disenchantment.

It is not only in the dimension of social space, however, that *Vanity Fair's* inscription of the new experience of an industrialized capitalist culture can be felt. For Thackeray, the ambiguous character of the commodity – its association with both pleasure and death – is perhaps more clearly illustrated by the temporal logic of fashion. Walter Benjamin believed that fashion (or 'novelty') took on the role of allegory within the cultural experience of the nineteenth century.[16] This idea is exemplified by the modern allegory of *Vanity Fair*, in which the cycle of fashion provides one of the principal instruments of Thackeray's exposition of the insubstantiality of material possessions, as well as one of the main targets of his satire on the folly of social pretension. Becky Sharp, for instance, is an embodiment not simply of the desire to acquire wealth and social status, but also, more precisely, of the display of fashionable commodities. To her son, Rawdon minor, she exhibits a grotesque resemblance to an animated fashion-plate:

> She came in like a vivified figure out of the *Magasin des Modes* – blandly smiling in the most beautiful new clothes and little gloves and boots. Wonderful scarfs, laces, and jewels glittered about her. She had always a new bonnet on: and flowers bloomed perpetually

> in it: or else magnificent curling ostrich feathers, soft and snowy as camellias. (*VF* 477)

Fashionable dress forms part of the armoury of Becky's performative self-presentation, just as it marks her subjection to sexual commodification by Lord Steyne. The shifting nature of fashion assists in her capacity to manipulate the visual effects of her appearance, often with deceptive intention. Yet fashion is not only equated with the performance (or construction) of 'femininity' in the novel, as the equally fashion-conscious figure of Jos Sedley illustrates. The self-exhibition of the dandy – a male creature of fashion – is just as reliant upon a preoccupation with clothing as that of any fashionable lady. It is this wilfully superficial and theatrical aspect of Thackeray's representation of fashionable society that led Robert Bell, one of *Vanity Fair's* reviewers, to characterize the novel as 'a lie from first to last . . . a movable *wardrobe*, without hearts or understandings beneath' (emphasis added) – a description that is highly perceptive, on the one hand, but seemingly oblivious to its satirical purpose on the other (*CH* 63–4). *Vanity Fair is*, indeed, a novel of two-dimensional surfaces in which any evidence for the existence of internal characteristics may also, deceptively, be a matter of appearances.

The logic of fashion dictates that commodities are inherently defined by their existence within time, and, therefore, that they are destined to become outmoded from the very moment of their production. Accordingly, Thackeray's narrator chooses the moment when Becky has reached the height of her success within fashionable society – her appearance at the court of King George IV – to remind his readers that fashions soon go out of date:

> Our beloved Rebecca had no need, however, of any such a friendly halo to set off her beauty. Her complexion could bear any sunshine as yet; and her dress, though if you were to see it now, any present lady of Vanity Fair would pronounce it to be the most foolish and preposterous attire ever worn, was as handsome in her eyes and those of the public, some five-and-twenty years since, as the most brilliant costume of the most famous beauty of the present season. A score of years hence that, too, that milliner's wonder, will have passed into the domain of the absurd, along with all previous vanities. (*VF* 601–2)

Becky's moment of triumph is rendered hollow by its exposure to the retrospective knowledge of the future, which convicts her fashionable appearance of absurdity. Yet the ridicule that is customarily extended to an outmoded fashion is forced to become self-reflexive. Just as the narrator reveals the future obsolescence of Becky's fashion, so he predicts the same fate for any reader who would be tempted to mock her. The future will repeat the same judgement upon the present as the present has on the past, and so on *ad infinitum*. The point of this narratorial aside is clear: fashion is the process by which each 'new' generation claims to distinguish itself from the old, and yet in so doing reveals an absolute inability to escape it. Though fashion is ostensibly predicated upon the desire for novelty, it is secretly defined by its unceasing repetition of the past. Through a narrative technique of temporal dislocation, Thackeray demonstrates that the desire instilled by fashion is thus predisposed to end in dissatisfaction.

This demonstration is, in fact, close to the stated aim with which Thackeray wrote the ending of *Vanity Fair*. In a letter to his critic Robert Bell, dated 3 September 1848, he declared: 'I want to leave everybody dissatisfied and unhappy at the end of the story – we ought all to be with our own and all other stories' (*LPP* ii. 423). Echoing the famous final paragraph of the novel, this statement perhaps suggests that, for Thackeray, stories themselves resemble the cultural experience of fashion, inciting our desire for novelty through their manipulation of the resources of narrative only to leave us with a familiar sense of disappointment at the unfulfilled promise of their endings. As a story itself, the form of *Vanity Fair* might, then, be said to coincide with the numerous individual narratives of disappointed desire that it contains. Given that it was conceived as both an immanent satire on the fashionable society of the early nineteenth century and a parody of the genre of the fashionable novel that claimed to represent it, this correspondence can, of course, be seen as appropriate. Fashion, however, is not the only name for the experience of the inevitable disappointment of desire in Thackeray's fiction, just as the form of the commodity does not provide its sole understanding of the material world; as I suggest in the following chapter, *realism is* another name for both.

3

Truthful Illusions: Thackeray's Realism

On its publication in volume form in 1848 *Vanity Fair* met with an interestingly divided response from contemporary reviewers. Whereas some critics, such as Robert Bell, recognized the theatrical and allegorical aspects of Thackeray's text, commenting on its resemblance to 'the conduct of a masquerade' , or 'movable wardrobe', wherein characters are shown in the act of assuming the duplicitous guises necessary for social performance (*CH* 63–4), others were more struck by the novel's realism, by its fidelity to 'nature'. G. H. Lewes, for instance, praised Thackeray for the 'strong sense of reality pervading his writing', and claimed that 'there was nothing theatrical in his manner': 'Life, not the phantasmagoria of the stage and circulating library, is the storehouse from whence he draws' (*CH* 48). A similar, though more troubled, perception was voiced by Elizabeth Rigby in a *Quarterly Review* article, which became notorious for its attack on the morality of a contemporaneous work of fiction, Charlotte Brontë's *Jane Eyre*. '*Vanity Fair*', wrote Rigby, 'is pre-eminently a novel of the day – not in the vulgar sense, of which there are too many, but as a literal photograph of the manners and habits of the nineteenth century, thrown on to paper by the light of a powerful mind' (*CH* 86). This difference of interpretation between some of Thackeray's earliest readers – between those who emphasized the performative virtuosity, or artfulness, of his fiction and those who saw primarily its mimetic faculty for realistic representation of contemporary (and earlier) social manners – responds to an ambivalence in his own conception of the nature of fictional illusion, which has continued to provoke critical debate. Though Thackeray is still commonly described as one of the great Victorian realist novelists, the character of his 'realism' is by no means easily defined.

'THE SENTIMENT OF REALITY'

Vanity Fair famously concludes with an acknowledgement of the illusory nature of fiction, which helps to ensure that readers finish the novel in a doubly disillusioned state. Not only do we learn that none of the characters in whose lives we have been interested finds happiness or satisfaction in gaining the object of his or her desires (an eventuality with most immediate reference to Dobbin's marriage to Amelia), but also that none of the characters is real anyway, and so our very disappointment is bereft of consolation: 'Come, children, let us shut up the box and the puppets, for our play is played out' (*VF* 878). To readers of the volume form of *Vanity Fair*, as distinct from the original monthly serial, the implication that the novel's characters are no more than 'puppets' to be manipulated at will by the author of the text comes, of course, as no surprise. In 'Before the Curtain', the prefatory text written retrospectively on completion of the serial narrative, Thackeray develops the metaphor of authorial puppetry more extensively, thus advertising, in advance, the unreality of his 'realism'. Adopting the persona of a puppet-master, or 'Manager of the Performance', who 'is proud to think that his Puppets have given satisfaction to the very best company in this empire' (*VF* 2), he openly draws attention to the artifice of his fictional performance, or, to put it the other way, seeks to deny his fiction's status as mimetic illusion. Readers who approach the novel with the simple expectation or desire of consuming an illusion can be discomforted by the narrator's references to the 'famous little Becky Puppet', the 'Amelia Doll', and the 'Dobbin Figure' (*VF* 2). In 'Before the Curtain', readers are effectively warned that a naively 'realistic' response to fictional illusion will lead to self-deception, just as the artful performance of Becky Sharp deceives gullible characters such as Jos Sedley within the fiction itself.

One solution to the apparent contradiction between *Vanity Fair's* open acknowledgement of artifice and its apparently successful illusion of reality would be to argue that what is most 'real', in terms of Thackeray's representation of nineteenth-century social manners, is precisely its insistent theatricality. The narrator's self-conscious exhibition of a fictive world comprised of shows, masks, puppets, and performances can be located in the historical context of emerging forms of cultural and commercial spectacle, as suggested in the previous chapter. Hence, one could view the performative language of *Vanity Fair* as a mirror accurately reflecting the social content of its satire. But more general ethical and aesthetic questions are also raised by Thackeray's wilful exposure of the mechanisms of fictional illusion (an exposure of the puppet wires, so to speak). As Barbara Hardy and, more recently, Alison Byerly have pointed out, one paradoxical effect of this technique can be to make Thackeray's fiction seem more, not less, realistic.[1] Given that the illusion engendered by even the most realistic of realist fictions is, in the most literal sense, untrue, a novel that reminds us of this prosaic fact lays claim to a greater degree of 'truth' or 'reality'. This argument can be employed as a defence against the criticism that came to be directed at the supposedly 'obtrusive' narrative voice by later writers working within the nineteenth-century realist tradition, most notably Henry James. Whereas James, in his influential essay 'The Art of Fiction' (1884), criticized Thackeray's disciple Anthony Trollope for employing a narrative voice that betrayed the fact that his fiction was only 'making believe',[2] Thackeray might well have replied that a conception of the novel as an autotelic medium of aesthetic illusion, equivalent in its denial of external fabrication to the writing of history itself, is only a more dishonest (since concealed) form of make-believe.

The obtrusiveness of the narrative voice in *Vanity Fair*, as in all Thackeray's subsequent novels, has often been a target for literary criticism influenced by James, especially in the early-to-mid twentieth century. But, strictly speaking, this voice is neither simply that of an 'omniscient', Godlike author, who assumes complete knowledge of all aspects of his fictive text, nor that of an author whose omniscience is proved through arbitrary violation of the illusion that he has created. Rather, Thackeray's narratorial personae are multiple in number and protean in form. In *Vanity Fair*, the perspective of the narrator constantly shifts between that of an internal participant in the fictive illusion, at moments becoming a 'character' with personal knowledge of other characters within the Fair, and that of an external observer and commentator, who himself assumes many different guises: the theatrical impresario, the clown, the preacher, the storyteller, as well as the omniscient author who claims 'the privilege of peeping into Miss Amelia Sedley's bedroom' (*VF* 185). Moreover, the narrator frequently addresses the reader as if he or she was also a familiar participant in the world of 'Vanity Fair', thus again blurring the boundary between 'real' and 'illusory' realms. While, in one sense, both narrator and reader are drawn inside the illusory world of the text, acquiring fictionalized identities in the process, in another, the illusion itself is presented as merely an extension of extra-textual reality, a quotidian world already known to the reader. Thackeray, in other words, does not attempt to create an inviolable aesthetic illusion, which exists at a secure distance from (though in imitation of) empirical reality. His inconsistent adoption of immanent and transcendent (internal and external) narratorial positions works to destabilize the ontological status of fiction, forcing readers to question and adapt their own modes of perception accordingly.

It is, nevertheless, important to note that Thackeray strongly supported those contemporary interpretations of his fiction that saw it primarily as an exposition of the doctrine of literary realism. In a letter to the critic David Masson, responding to his comparative review of Dickens's *David Copperfield* and *Pendennis* (both published in 1850), Thackeray agreed with the suggestion that, of the two writers, Dickens manifested the greater capacity for imaginative and fanciful invention whereas he came closer to representing the 'natural' in art. Though professing admiration for Dickens, he 'protest[s] against' the unreality of a figure such as Micawber, 'holding that the Art of Novels is to represent Nature: to convey as strongly as possible the sentiment of reality'. Alluding, moreover, to the way in which familiar objects are metaphorically transformed into the extraordinary or grotesque by Dickens's language, Thackeray expresses the view that 'in a drawing-room drama a coat is a coat and a poker a poker; and must be nothing else according to my ethics, not an embroidered tunic, nor a great red-hot instrument like the Pantomime weapon' (*CH* 128). The faithful representation of these humble material objects is viewed as an important aspect of the moral responsibility of fiction, or, to be more specific, of bourgeois realist fiction (the 'drawing-room drama'), as distinct from 'tragedy' or other more elevated cultural forms. The realist novel, this suggests, should not seek to transfigure the quotidian familiarity of its object-world through the imaginative resources of language, but, rather, to insist on an absolute transparency of meaning between the object and its linguistic sign, remaining, as far as possible, *within* the material environment that it claims to reproduce.

However, as Jack Rawlins has observed, Thackeray's valorization of the 'sentiment of reality' is essentially a moral stance towards the writing of fiction, which does not prescribe any determinate aesthetic or linguistic form.[3] For this reason, it is important to differentiate Thackeray's realism from the more self-conscious and programmatic literary movement that developed under the same title later in the nineteenth century, both as a quasi-scientific discipline (in the guise of Zola's 'Naturalism' and George Eliot's later novels), on the one hand, and as a type of aestheticism (in the cases of Flaubert and James), on the other. Thackeray's insistence on truth to 'Nature', for example, derives primarily from his knowledge of eighteenth-century literary debate, and holds more in common with Fielding than it does with Zola. The opinion expressed in his letter to David Masson is, in fact, a recapitulation of an argument already outlined in the Preface to *Pendennis*, where he cites Fielding's *Tom Jones* (1749) as an example of the 'Natural in our Art', which the contemporary Victorian public is unwilling to 'tolerate' (*P.*, p. lvi). Just as Fielding had sought to distinguish the 'truth' of his own fictional history from the 'idle romances' with which it was forced to compete in the literary marketplace,[4] so Thackeray, a century later, uses his preface to distance *Pendennis* from the degrading 'excitement' offered by gothic romance and melodrama, and asks the reader 'to believe that this person writing strives to tell the truth' (*P.*,

p. lvi). At its most basic level, then, realism, for Thackeray, can be defined as a mode of fictional discourse that aims to become 'truthful' by countering the merely conventional, or at worst duplicitous and morally corrupting, forms of 'romance': hence, its accommodation of the cognate form of parody in both Thackeray and Fielding. Yet Thackeray is aware that realism itself attracts conventional moral censure in seeking to expose the dubious morality that it finds in other types of fiction. His preface to *Pendennis* insinuates that he would have liked to go further in recording the sexual experiences of Arthur Pendennis, who is envisaged as a typical middle-class 'gentleman' of his generation, 'no better nor worse than most educated men', but laments that the pressure of social respectability does not permit him to 'depict to his utmost power a MAN' (*P.*, p. lvi). Though Thackeray claims that a 'little more frankness than is customary has been attempted in this story', he acknowledges that the possibility of a truthful representation of contemporary social manners is limited in scope by comparison with the realism of his eighteenth-century predecessor (*P.*, p. lvii).

It is also from Fielding, in part, that Thackeray takes the demystifying, anti-heroic rhetoric of his truth-telling fiction, although the ideas of heroism and hero worship acquire a new cultural significance in the wake of Carlyle's writings of the 1840s. If *Vanity Fair is* strikingly (and ambiguously) subtitled *A Novel without a Hero*, the central figure of *Pendennis is* equally devoid of the conventional attributes of a romantic hero, and the same is true of the young male protagonists of the two novels subsequently narrated by Pendennis, *The Newcomes* and *The Adventures of Philip.* In each of the three latter texts, the place of the 'hero' is occupied by a typical representative of the middle-class man of the world: an *homnie moyen sensuel*, or gentleman of average ability and inconsistent moral principle, who, as Thackeray says of Pendennis, 'does not claim to be a hero, but only a man and a brother' (*P.* 977). Another defining characteristic of the realism of Thackeray's fiction, then, is its implicit association of the 'natural' or 'truthful' in art with a fundamentally bourgeois mode of experience – one that generally seeks to avoid both elevated and vulgar extremes in form and subject matter. At least in so far as the later novels are concerned, the ordinary, unheroic 'reality' of bourgeois life comes to form the ideological substratum of the widely acknowledged verisimilitude of his fiction, in accordance with his declared preference for the 'honesty' of the '*bourgeois* style of art' in painting over Romantic or neo-classical sublimities (*WMT* xiii. 371).

FABLES OF DISENCHANTMENT

Following the success of *Vanity Fair*, Thackeray's fiction of the 1850s continues to develop a practice of literary realism that works, principally, as an agent of disenchantment and disillusionment in the most literal meaning of the words. Defined through negation, the truthful realism of this fiction emerges through its cumulative exposition of the dangerous delusions engendered by the pursuit of treasured ideals. At the same time, this process is problematized by an intermittent awareness that the discourse of realist fiction is itself another form of illusion, or fable. The trilogy of novels featuring Arthur Pendennis as first 'hero' and then narrator constitutes a coherent and interrelated body of work, whose more or less contemporary historical settings can also, conveniently, be distinguished from the self-consciously 'historical' novels written by Thackeray during the same decade. Coincidence of historical setting and characters are not the only means of establishing the coherence of this group of texts, but neither are they superficial considerations in this instance. The device of continuing the same characters from novel to novel – an idea probably borrowed from Balzac and, in turn, borrowed from Thackeray by Trollope – became an increasingly settled habit with Thackeray from the composition of *Pendennis* onwards, and in the Pendennis trilogy, especially, it serves an important mimetic function. Pen's narration of the life stories of his friends Clive Newcome and Philip Firmin not only supports the fiction of his personal development as a writer, established in *Pendennis*, but, more generally, helps to create the illusion of an organically interconnected textual world, extending beyond the artificial boundaries that demarcate the beginnings and endings of individual narratives, and thus appearing to reflect the open-ended narrative experience of lived reality itself.

Alongside Pen, numerous characters from *Pendennis* (Warrington, Laura, Major Pendennis, Captain Costigan) and from earlier texts (Becky Sharp, Dobbin, Lord Steyne, Caroline Gann, Dr Firmin) make appearances, however brief or oblique, in *The Newcomes* and *Philip.* Paradoxically, the more Thackeray's habit of self-referential quotation shows his fiction to be densely intertextual, each novel acquiring meaning through its reconstitution of a network of pre-existing texts, the more 'true to life' it seems.

On the other hand, the recurrence of the same characters within successive texts casts an impression of uniformity, rather than of heterogeneity, upon the three Pendennis novels. Though each of the novels invokes the richness of an imagined world that cannot be contained within the boundaries of a single text, it also signals the retelling of an essentially familiar story. In addition to the literal repetition of redeploying some of his previous characters, Thackeray invents new characters whose resemblance to their predecessors is only reinforced by their fictive coexistence. As I have already noted, Clive Newcome and Philip Firmin are both variations on the figure of Arthur Pendennis, and thus the decision to make Pen the narrator and confidant of their experience creates a curious doubling effect within each of the texts: on each occasion, more or less the same story is retold by a character who is known to have already undergone it. The narrative design initiated in *Pendennis*, and subsequently reworked in *The Newcomes* and *Philip*, should be placed in the context of the important nineteenth-century genre of the *Bildungsroman*, or novel of education, inaugurated by Goethe in *Wilhelm Meister's Apprenticeship* (1795–6). In its most rudimentary form, the term *Bildungsroman* designates a type of narrative that traces the development of the individual self from immature to mature consciousness, commonly proceeding from a state of innocence and naivety, as embodied in the period of early life, to one of experience, self-knowledge, and, in some cases, reconcilation with the external world. Thackeray gives a somewhat parochial inflection to this paradigm by focusing specifically upon the 'education' of the young, bourgeois gentleman as he emerges from adolescence into adulthood, and struggles to accommodate individual desires within a prescribed class and gender identity. Moreover, each of the three novels incorporates substantial autobiographical material from Thackeray's own personal and professional history in a relatively transparent form: *Pendennis*, as we have seen, records the rites of passage of a writer, as does *Philip* to a lesser extent, while *The New-emes* follows Clive's progress as an artist, a career also considered by the young Thackeray. The range of cultural and psychological experience represented within these texts thus remains homogeneous, perhaps even to the point of self-obsession.

Pendennis provides the clearest, most sustained, example of Thackeray's appropriation of the genre of the *Bildungsroman*. A third-person biographical narrative charts the history of Pen's experience through successive stages of development, from naive schoolboy to dissipated university student, from Romantic poet to hack journalist, culminating in the respectability of a career in politics. The process of this narrative is clearly educative in the required generic sense, but what is learned is primarily negative in character: following Balzac, it becomes a story of 'lost illusions', or, to use Georg Lukács's classification, a novel of 'romantic disillusionment'.' Pen's youthful infatuation with the actress named the Fotheringay is one of the first and best examples of this unsentimental course of education. As in *Vanity Fair*, theatricality (and, specifically, the performance of femininity) is deceptively alluring to the male spectator, and Pen's worship of the actress illustrates, in a fairly benign form, the perils of succumbing to theatrical illusion. It is Pen's susceptibility to the power of aesthetic illusion that leads to his unconscious participation in the construction of her 'beautiful image': 'He supplied the meaning which her words wanted; and created the divinity which he loved' (*P.* 67). Thackeray's narrative voice, however, is able to reveal the reality that belies the illusion of theatrical performance as the Fotheringay walks off stage:

> And after she had come out trembling with emotion before the audience, and looking so exhausted and tearful that you fancied she would faint with sensibility, she would gather up her hair the instant she was behind the curtain, and go home to a mutton-chop and a glass of brown stout; and the harrowing labours of the day

> over, she went to bed and snored as resolutely and as regularly as a porter. (*P.* 73)

This is one of numerous occasions in the text when the narrator forces upon the reader his apprehension of the 'contrast between practice and poetry' (*P.* 301), an ironic awareness of the absurd disjunction between the deluded idealism of youth and the prosaic materiality of the world as it stands: a world that the adult consciousness must learn to recognize, if not simply to accept, for what it is. As the novel develops, Pen's maturation allows him to share in the knowledge of the 'Cynical philosophy' that the narrating consciousness possesses from the start (*P.* 301). Thus, he learns that artistic 'sensibility' – a keyword in the passage quoted above – is capable of being manufactured at will, as the fate of his own poetry and that of Blanche Amory (whose book of poems is mockingly entitled *Mes Lames)* also testifies. The seemingly spontaneous and unmediated expression of emotion celebrated in the poetics of sensibility is perhaps the most egregious example of the duplicity of aesthetic illusion, since it cloaks the artifice of its performance in a rhetoric of sincerity – a fact that becomes apparent when Pen composes poetry for the Fotheringay, but later readdresses it to Blanche.

Poetic sensibility is shown to be doubly inauthentic, more over, because of its status as a commodity in the market society of *Pendennis*. Pen's initiation into the literary-journalistic trade performs the most striking act of disenchantment within the text, for it reveals that the very substance of the novel that Thackeray is writing – the medium of language itself – participates in an illusionistic dissimulation of the material reality of its production. None of the writings of the various journalists and literary hacks encountered by Pen is quite what it appears to be: Captain Shandon's address on behalf of the 'gentlemen of England' in his prospectus for the *Pall Mall Gazette is* composed in a debtor's prison by an impecunious Irishman (*P.* 409), whilst the vehement political opinions of Tory and Radical newspapers are manufactured indifferently by hired journalists. The aura that surrounds 'literature' in the mind of the uninitiated is quickly dispelled on closer acquaintance with the machinations of the literary trade. This process is later exemplified when Warrington advises Pen on how to rewrite *Walter Lorraine* – his novel of lachrymose Romantic sensibility – for commercial publication: 'give him a more modern air, prune away, though sparingly, some of the green passages, and add a little comedy, and cheerfulness, and satire, and that sort of thing, and then we'll take him to market and sell him' (*P.* 523). The act of self-commodification that is embodied in the revision of Pen's autobiography is symbolically central to the novel's examination of the corrosive effects of an increasingly commercialized culture on the moral integrity of the individual. As Warrington is aware, the selling of *Walter Lorraine is* akin to an act of prostitution on the part of the 'comely lad' who represents both Pen and his fictional surrogate, and perhaps also Thackeray himself, whose own youthful autobiographical experience is on sale within his text (*P.* 523).

The question of whether Pen's self-commodification will extend to a marriage of convenience with Blanche Amory continues the theme of prostitution within the narrative, but Thackeray characteristically undermines the simplistic moral opprobium in which it is conventionally couched. Chapter LXIV, entitled 'Temptation', for example, concludes with an ironically self-implicating exclamation, which recognizes the author's collusion in the ethical frailty shown by his protagonist: 'And if every woman and man in this kingdom, who has sold her or himself for money or position, as Mr Pendennis was about to do, would but purchase a copy of his memoirs, what tons of volumes Messrs Bradbury and Evans would sell!' (*P.* 839). Here, Thackeray exposes the parallel between Pen's fictive occupation as a producer of literary commodities and the reality of his own corresponding situation in a way that goes beyond that of simple autobiographical representation. While recognizing the moral inadequacy of Pen's increasingly cynical acquiescence in the commodification of literature and life, he simultaneously questions the possibility of standing in judgement over it. There is no untainted moral vantage point offered within the text from which Pen's worldly prudence could be condemned, neither that of the narrator, whose 'Cynical Philosophy' is the very content of his education, nor that of the idealized female figures, Laura and Pen's mother

Helen, who stand at the opposite extreme. In the words of the narrator, *Pendennis is* a 'Selfish Story', within which 'almost every person, according to his nature . . . and according to the way of the world as it seems to us, is occupied about Number One' (*P.* 719–20); and, while selfishness is certainly a moral failing, it is also, he implies, the inevitable corollary of a culture in which the universal commodification of objects of desire reduces the experience of the individual self to that of an isolated and acquisitive consumer. One of the recurrent themes of narratorial digression in the novel concerns the existential solitariness of the individual within the crowded condition of society: 'you and I are but a pair of infinite isolations, with some fellow-islands a little more or less near to us', the narrator informs the reader on one occasion (*P.* 184). The selfishness of the isolated ego, in other words, is by no means a unique moral deviancy perpetrated by Pen, but, rather, a pathology endemic to the 'way of the world' that he is taken to embody.

This is not to suggest that *Pendennis* succeeds in expunging all traces of conventional moral sentiment from its analysis of existing worldly reality. If the narrator refrains from adopting a superior moral position to the novel's 'hero', neither can he remain comfortable with a process of disenchantment that culminates in a merely convenient acquiescence in the law of material self-interest. Hence, the 'illusions' entertained by the youthful Pen are never truly lost, but, instead, transposed to the realm of memory, where they survive, in renewed form, as objects of nostalgia. The retrospective biographical form of the narrative ensures that the impulse to move forward, developmentally, in time is always in tension with the desire to recollect an idealized past. For this reason, Thackeray's commitment to the genre of the *Bildungsroman is* incomplete: there is a sense in which Pen's identity, like all others according to the narrator, always remains as it was in the beginning. A similar ambivalence can be witnessed in the representation of the two women who do most to remind Pen of his abandoned moral integrity. While the narrator does not entirely exempt Pen's mother from his observations upon the selfish motivation of atomized human desires, she, along with Laura, stands as an embodiment of the capacity for self-sacrificial love, which is sentimentally ascribed to women. Laura and Helen occupy a space within the novel – the domestic sphere of Fairoaks – that is physically, as well as culturally and psychologically, removed from the public world that Pen, as a young middle-class gentleman, desires (but is also forced) to enter. Thus, alongside the temporal domain of childhood and adolescence, the spatial domain of women is equated with a moral and aesthetic idealism that is alternately praised and derided by the male voices of the text. Like Agnes Wickfield *in David Copperfield,* Laura assumes the role of moral conscience within the life of the male protagonist, though, unlike Dickens, Thackeray cannot help implying that the angelic virtue of the domestic female may also be a symptom of her self-delusion.

In *The Newcomes,* the focus of narrative disenchantment is split, more or less evenly, between the story of Clive Newcome's doomed romantic love for his cousin Ethel and Colonel Newcome's admirable, but outmoded, ideal of the conduct of a true 'gentleman'. The former corresponds more closely to the model of the negative *Bildungsroman* established in *Pendennis,* with Thackeray tracing the course of Clive's emotional experience, alongside the development of his professional career as an artist, from adolescence to early adulthood. In some respects, Clive can be seen as a morally purified substitute for Pen, a figure whose experience of the world teaches disillusionment, but which casts him in the light of a suffering martyr to romantic ideals, rather than as the alternately shrewd and complacent cynic of the earlier novel. Unlike the unheroic hero of *Pendennis,* Clive is 'just such a youth as has a right to be the hero of a novel' (*NC* 75), although his vocation as an artist is by no means idealized, as we shall come to see. The failure of Clive's romantic aspirations, however, is tied to a polemic against the commercialization of contemporary bourgeois and aristocratic manners, which extends the theme of prostitution from *Pendennis.* What prohibits the union of Clive and Ethel within the realist space of fictional illusion that precedes the shift to an acknowledgement of fiction as wish-fulfilment (or pure illusion) in the final chapter, is the brutal logic of the system of cultural and economic exchange that regulates marriage amongst the 'respectable' classes of early

Victorian society. As Lord Kew points out, Clive's dream of 'love in a cottage' (*NC* 392) stands no chance of realization within a social formation whose pursuit of the ideal alliance of aristocratic cultural distinction and bourgeois economic security is thoroughly self-conscious. But, while Clive lacks the necessary economic and cultural capital to buy Ethel's hand in marriage, it is the latter who is shown to suffer the greater consequences of her internalized desire for social status. As a woman on the marriage market, Ethel accepts the reality of her status as a commodity, an object of barter and exchange between two patriarchal families, whereas Clive, as a male suitor, has at least the possibility of expressing a disinterested love. Some of Thackeray's most direct and impassioned satire in *The Newcomes* is directed against the trafficking of women in respectable society, which he often likens to the customs of 'savage' nations: the Oriental harem and the practice of Suttee, suppressed by the British in India.

Arguably, the more striking case of disillusionment within *The Newcomes*, however, centres upon Colonel Newcome, a figure whom Victorian readers tended to view as the real hero of the novel. In the opening dramatic scene, set in the 'Cave of Harmony' tavern, the Colonel immediately strikes an inharmonious note by interrupting Captain Costigan's ribald song with the words: 'I thought I was coming to a society of gentlemen' (*NC* 13). This initial rebuke is prophetic of the Colonel's indictment of 'society' in a much larger sense than is designated by its immediate context. The question of what constitutes a 'society of gentlemen', and in what ways gentlemanliness is missing from the society of the 1820s to 1840s that the novel depicts, is most explicitly addressed through its examination of the values represented by Colonel Newcome. From the outset of this enquiry, Thackeray makes it clear that the Colonel's idea of the gentleman is, to a large extent, a fictional creation, modelled on a selective appreciation of the heroes of seventeenth- and eighteenth-century literature: Cervantes's Don Quixote, Richardson's Sir Charles Grandison, and *The Spectator's* Sir Roger de Coverley. These characters, he believes, are 'the finest gentlemen in the world', and the pleasure of reading their texts comes from the desire 'to be in the company of gentlemen' (*NC* 49). The Colonel's disappointment at the absence of the gentleman in nineteenth-century society is, thus, at one level, simply an inevitable consequence of his naive expectation of locating an anachronistic fictional ideal within a new historical reality – another illustration of what the narrator of *Pendennis* calls the 'contrast between practice and poetry'. As Robin Gilmour has observed, it is significant that the Colonel objects to the 'low' comedy of *Tom Jones*, in Thackeray's terms a more 'truthful' (because ambiguous) eighteenth-century model of gentlemanly character.[6] Yet, although Thackeray's representation of the Colonel's deluded idealism is clearly ironic, he is also deeply sympathetic with its challenge to the cultural values of 'modern' society. In this respect, *The Newcomes* is, indeed, an updated version of the Don Quixote myth: a story in which the Colonel's anachronistic chivalric code of gentlemanliness functions as a barometer of cultural change, eliciting a mixture of admiration and ridicule. Ironically, as in the case of *Don Quixote*, readers of *The Newcomes* have tended to neglect the latter, more satirical, aspects of Thackeray's characterization of Colonel Newcome, thus leading both to the sentimentalized figure celebrated by Victorian critics, such as Trollope, and the reaction against this figure in twentieth-century criticism. A telling detail from the text, which belies this one-sided reading, is the reference in chapter XXII to a fictitious painting in the Royal Academy that 'treats us to a subject from the best of all stories, the tale "which laughed Spain's chivalry away", the ever new *Don Quixote*' (*NC* 278).

If the ambivalence surrounding the figure of Colonel Newcome is one example of the difficulty of reading the disillusioned, satirical tone of *The Newcomes*, another would be the treatment of 'art' within the novel. In *Pendennis*, the trade of literature is shown to be concerned with the production of *illusion in* the most negative, ideological sense of the word: the illusion being, precisely, that literature is not concerned with trade. By comparison, in *The Newcomes*, the profession of art holds out the utopian possibility of a genuinely alternative world of illusion, whilst reflecting the realistic probability of its entanglement with the degraded world of commerce. This ambivalence is dramatized through the explicitly contrasted careers of Clive Newcome and J. J. Ridley. Whereas Clive is no more than a talented and enthusiastic copyist from nature, J.J. is distinguished by his capacity for imaginative invention. As Clive ruefully confesses: 'I can beat him in drawing horses, I know, and dogs; but I can only draw what I see. Somehow he seems to see things we don't, don't you know?' (*NC* 166). Moreover, as the following passage demonstrates, whilst Clive is merely a gentleman-amateur artist, who struggles to free himself from the established aristocratic prejudice against the single-minded pursuit of art as a vocation, J.J. exemplifes the virtues of self-discipline, application and the capacity for labour associated with a new middle-class professionalism:

> But was the young gentleman always at the drawing-board copying from the antique when his father supposed him to be so devotedly engaged? I fear his place was sometimes vacant. His friend J.J. worked every day, and all day. Many a time the steady little student remarked his patron's absence, and no doubt gently remonstrated with him; but when Clive did come to his work, he executed it with remarkable skill and rapidity . . . (*NC* 232)

The tone with which the narrator distinguishes, here, between the dilettantish 'young gentleman' and the 'steady little student' might suggest that the contrast between them is not quite as invidious to Clive as it first appears. Throughout the novel, J.J. is described in strangely diminutive, even infantilizing, terms, as if the gentlemanly narrator were colluding in the patronizing affection of his friend Clive. Yet, as the narrative wears on, it becomes increasingly clear that the gentlemanly prejudice against the professional artist is also one of the targets of Thackeray's irony. J.J.'s praise of Clive's talent as a portrait-painter, that 'he had the art of seizing the likeness, and of making all his people look like gentlemen' (*NC* 642), pays testimony to an underlying soundness of moral principle perhaps, but is a less than overwhelming verdict on his imaginative power as an artist. Although Clive's decision to pursue his artistic vocation is itself perceived as an act of defiance against the stifling demands of bourgeois respectability, the mediocrity of his talent ensures that his art is never in danger of transcending the narrow confines of his class identity. By the end of the novel, his speciality in portraiture is viewed as a branch of artistic practice that reproduces existing hierarchies of social and economic power, rather than asserting the independence of the artist.

In contrast, the figure of J. J. Ridley is situated within an artistic idyll, uncontaminated by the insidiously corrupting forces of the 'world':

> The palette on his arm was a great shield painted of many colours: he carried his maul-stick and a sheaf of brushes along with it, the weapons of his glorious but harmless war. With these he achieves conquests, wherein none are wounded save the envious: with that he shelters him against how much idleness, ambition, temptation! Occupied over that consoling work, idle thoughts cannot gain the mastery over him: selfish wishes or desires are kept at bay. Art is truth: and truth is religion: and its study and practice a daily work of pious duty. What are the world's struggles, brawls, successes, to that calm recluse pursuing his calling? (*NC* 850–1)

This is a highly unusual gesture for Thackeray: an apparently unironic assertion of the capacity of art to transcend worldly desires, offering 'shelter' and 'consolation' in response to the fierce self-interest of society, and exuding the sanctity of religious truth. Evidently, Thackeray uses J.J. to personify a 'purer' form of artistic practice than Clive is capable of attaining, but this makes him a somewhat unconvincing figure in terms of the novel's social realism. The romanticized notion of art as a refuge from material reality is, appropriately enough, invoked as an abstract and ethereal vision within the text, strangely at odds with the central thrust of its narrative exposition. A more characteristic example of Thackeray's apprehension of the condition of art within bourgeois society would be the memorably ironic episode in chapter XXVIII, in which Ethel fashions herself into a *tableau vivant* of painting 'number 46 in the Exhibition of the Gallery of Painters in Water-colours' (*NC* 362) by pinning a green ticket to her dress, and thus displaying the sign of her purchase. Works of art, this episode suggests, occupy a similar status to women in being viewed primarily as objects of exchange within the commercial system that *The Newcomes* presents as all-pervasive.

Yet the seemingly naive celebration of J.J.'s pure artistic talent is also less incongruous than it first appears. As R. D. McMaster points out, J.J.'s association with imagination aligns him with the generic modes of romance and fantasy, which are also invoked by the narrative framework of *The Newcome's*.[7] What seems like a crudely infantilizing reference to the artist's residence in 'Fancy Street – Poetry Street – Imagination Street' (*NC* 154) makes more sense when we consider it alongside the generic mixture of children's fairy tale and Aesop's fable that comprises the 'overture' of chapter I and the return to 'fable-land' in the closing pages of the novel. At these boundary points within the text, Thackeray playfully exposes the labour of artistic imagination that underpins even the most apparently effortless mimetic illusions, hinting that the discourse of fictional realism is only one amongst a number of different generic codes capable of embodying the same 'farrago of old fables' (*NC* 4). Thus, for example, the animal fable 'in which jackdaws . . . wear peacock's feathers' (*NC* 5) is not merely a fanciful prelude to the 'true' fictive world of the Newcomes, but, rather, an illustration of how the comedy of social emulation that the reader will shortly encounter within this world can be translated into a different code. As with the implausible figure of J. J. Ridley, then, Thackeray steps outside the conventions of realist fiction in order to demarcate its place within the larger context of human fabulation. This narrative strategy generates complex effects, suggesting, on the one hand, that the concrete particularity of realist fiction conceals an underlying conformity to the archetypal structure of the fable, while, on the other, enhancing the novel's claim to realism when it appears to depart from its scripted design. When, at the end of the narrative, for instance, Thackeray refuses to unite Clive and Ethel except in the nebulous realm of 'fable-land' (*NC* 1009), he exposes the normative 'happy ending' of Victorian fiction as little more than a degraded form of wish-fulfilment, but insinuates that his own fable carries a different message altogether. The authority of the creative artist in ordering the space of aesthetic illusion is recognized as both absolute and ineffectual: 'the poet of fable-land rewards and punishes absolutely. He splendidly deals out bags of sovereigns, which won't buy anything' (*NC* 1009). While Thackeray accepts this factitious aspect of his role as a writer of fables, he is simultaneously aware of its incapacity to represent the social and economic injustice experienced by his characters in fictive 'reality'. His solution, at the end of *The . . . Newcomes, is* to make explicit the tension between his desire for truthful illusion and his understanding that all illusion is untrue.

A similar strategy of ironic compliance with novelistic convention can be observed in the ending of *Philip,* the final novel in the Pendennis trilogy. Here, in a chapter entitled The Realms of Bliss', Thackeray makes the fairy-tale reversal of Philip Firmin's genteel poverty so extremely preposterous as to dispense with the necessity of registering a formal shift from realism to 'fable-land'. It is obvious to all but the most ingenuous of readers that the narrative culminates in a parodic mode that again satirizes the generic requirements of Victorian romance. The cynical irony of this ending, with its apparently weary acknowledgement that all novels lead mechanically to the 'realms of bliss', is characteristic of a narratorial posture that has often disturbed, irritated, or bored readers of *Philip.* It is in this text, along with the immediately preceding novella *Lovel the Widower* (1860), that Thackeray takes his sceptical interrogation of the mechanisms of fictional illusion to a logical, and tortuously self-deconstructive, extreme. The very idiosyncracy of *Philip,* however, makes it a fascinating text for readers interested in tracing the development of Thackeray's literary aesthetic, since it reveals in an exaggerated form the peculiar conception of realism that is evident in his fiction from *Vanity Fair* onwards.

Just as, in *The Newcomes,* Thackeray was conscious of reworking material from *Pendennis,* so, in *Philip,* he becomes even more painfully conscious of producing a repetition of a repetition. Thus, a recognition of the archetypal structure of fables is again set alongside the intimate particularity of contemporary domestic manners. Here, though, the juxtaposition of conflicting generic registers serves primarily to disrupt and display the formal mechanisms of plot development and character construction, rather than marking a thematic disjunction between 'realism' and 'fairy tale', as in *The Newcomes.* The narrator, for instance, manifests his 'disdain' for the 'artifice' of narrative suspense by interrupting his account of the troubled courtship of Philip and Charlotte to reassure readers that they are now, at the time of writing, an ageing and happily married couple (*WMT* xi. 375). Elsewhere, the mimetic surface of the text is peeled away to reveal the presence of a writer producing a novel for economic exchange:

> Ah! how wonderful ways and means are! When I think how this very line, this very word, which I am writing represents money, *I* am lost in a respectful astonishment . . . I am paid, we will say, for the sake of illustration, at the rate of sixpence per line. With the words 'Ah, how wonderful,' to the words 'per line,' I can buy a loaf, a piece of butter, a jug of milk, a modicum of tea, – actually enough to make breakfast for the family; and the servants of the house; and the charwoman, *their* servant, can shake up the tea-leaves with a fresh supply of water, sop the crusts, and get a meal *taut l'ien que mat*. Wife, children, guests, servants, charwoman, we are all actually making a meal off Philip Firmin's bones as it were. (*WMT* xi. 537)

In such passages as this, Thackeray radically demystifies the construction of mimetic illusion, demonstrating its basis in real material needs and desires. But, of course, this demystification is itself part of the illusion that his fiction seeks to create: the illusion that the writer figured here is real, and that by revealing his presence the text is not less, but more, realistic in essence. In *Philip*, Thackeray develops his long-standing recognition of the paradox of truth-telling fiction into a more sustained form of meta-fictional realism, which, historically at least, occupies a median point between the eighteenth-century practice of Lawrence Sterne and the 'postmodern' novel of the late twentieth century. Lacking the self-confident experimentalism of both earlier and later forms of meta-fiction, however, *Philip* works to corrode the basis of the reader's involvement in the narrative, whilst confessing its inability to transcend the threadbare cliches of Victorian melodrama.

DOMESTIC REALISM/FAMILY ROMANCE

The Pendennis trilogy constitutes Thackeray's most substantial contribution to the ideologically dominant mid-Victorian genre of fiction, the domestic realist novel. Yet in these novels the everyday drama of bourgeois domestic life is anything but comfortably reaffirmed. In addition to the formal and thematic resemblances that I have already considered, *Pendennis, The Newcomes,* and *Philip* are bound together by their common apprehension of the dysfunctional and disintegrative condition of the Victorian middle-class family, and of the intergenerational and gendered conflicts that mark its state of crisis. Each of the novels dramatizes a similar conflict between the aspirations of the young male protagonist and the inhibiting influence of an older generation, both maternal and paternal, whether explicitly malign or not. Arthur Pendennis, first of all, is torn between the opposing, though equally problematic, influences of his 'pure', but sexually possessive, mother and Major Pendennis, his 'corrupt', but indulgent, uncle, who becomes a surrogate father to him. This pattern is reconfigured *in The Newcomes,* where Clive is set in conflict with a 'good' father and Ethel with a 'bad' (step)mother (Lady Kew) – again, morally opposed figures who both exercise a harmful influence on the lives of their children. Finally, in *Philip,* the presence of a largely benign maternal figure (the Little Sister) only partially offsets the hero's revolt against a malevolent father (Dr Firmin). Within all of these novels, moreover, intergenerational conflict is presented as irresolvable, other than through the death, permanent exile, or extreme senescence of the parental figures. Thackeray's use of the form of the *Bildungsroman* in charting the development of the hero's mature consciousness is, thus, predicated on the necessity of the dissolution, and subsequent reconstitution, of the family for its successful resolution.

It is questionable whether a single individualist model of psychological trauma, along the lines of the Oedipal conflict, can be said to determine this narrative structure since both fathers and mothers are cast in an equally baleful light by the emotional trials of the young protagonists, just as dramatically different occupants of each role (Colonel Newcome and Dr Firmin, Helen Pendennis and Lady Kew) appear similarly harmful in their stewardship of youth. An alternative approach would be to read Thackeray's representations of individual development and intra-familial conflict as exemplifying a broader process of socio-historical change. The struggles of Pen, Clive, and Philip to emerge from the shackles of an oppressive familial environment could, perhaps, be taken to signify the collective experience of a generation of young

Victorian men, struggling to shape a new cultural identity in distinction from their immediate historical predecessors. What complicates this reading, however, is the fact that Thackeray's representation of 'modern' (i.e. Victorian) culture in the novels is by no means positive, as we have seen, and that it is precisely the anachronistic, pre-Victorian world of the older generations that tends to attract his nostalgic attachment. Whether it is through the stereotype of the worldly Regency dandy (Major Pendennis) or, conversely, the ingenuous eighteenth-century gentleman (Colonel Newcome), the cultural figures of the past overshadow the insipid forms of moralism and materialism that characterize the Victorian present, even when they cannot be perceived as ethically superior.

Where Thackeray's young gentlemen do succeed in locating a source of cultural identity to rival the aura of their elders is in their temporary escape from the oppressive respectability of the bourgeois family structure into the alternative social space of 'bohemia'. Although the Pendennis novels can be described as examples of mid-Victorian domestic realism, what is perhaps most appealing about these texts – at least for a certain category of contemporary reader, namely the young middle-class male whose vicarious desires the fictitious life of the protagonist can most immediately embody – is their tantalizing evocation of a subcultural world that exists outside of, but contiguous to, the normative spheres of family and work. In *Pendennis* and *Philip* this bohemian subculture centres around the semi-disreputable literary-journalistic communities of London and Paris, and in *The Newcomes* around a comparable society of artists. According to Eve Kosofsky Sedgwick, it was Thackeray, in his Pendennis fiction, who 'half invented for English literature and half merely housetrained' the idea of 'bohemia', originally developed in France: 'In these bachelor novels', she argues, 'the simple absence of an enforcing family structure was allowed to perform its enchantment in a more generalized way' than was to become the case for a later, more specifically homosexual, bohemian subculture.[8] If the bohemian passages of the lives of Thackeray's fictional protagonists do not signify an identifiable 'homosexual' attachment, they clearly do represent an experience of intense male comradeship, which is facilitated by a temporary loosening of family ties, as well as connoting a vaguely defined sexual transgressiveness. In each of the Pendennis novels, 'bohemia' is conceived as a space of male homosocial freedom encountered during the process of the hero's development, but ultimately (and regrettably) abandoned in his pursuit of wider social advancement and normative domestic 'bliss'.

The friendship between Pen and his fellow journalist George Warrington is perhaps the clearest embodiment of the truth of Sedgwick's observation. For much of *Pendennis,* the legal establishment in which the two bachelors jointly reside forms a liberating alternative 'domesticity' to the stifling matriarchal environment of Fairoaks, Pen's family home. Thackeray plays upon this analogy directly, not seeking to conceal it, by comically representing the domestic harmony of the two men in his visual illustrations for the text. At the same time, Pen's bachelor establishment provides the opportunity for his heartless seduction of the working-class girl, Fanny Bolton – an act that, though formally condemned from the narratorial viewpoint, signals the extent of his sexual freedom. Heterosexual transgression is not presented as incompatible with a heightened 'romantic' attachment to a male comrade. In *The Newcomes,* the affection that marks the homosocial bond between men is emphasized when the introduction of Clive, with 'a bronzed face, and a yellow beard and mustachios, and those bright cheerful eyes', humorously threatens to triangulate the intimacy between Pen and Warrington: 'if I could have found it in my heart to be jealous of such a generous brave fellow, I might have grudged him his share of Warrington's regard', Pen remarks (*NC* 523). The romantic allure of bohemia, however, is evoked more by the generic spaces of male community, to which the life of the bachelor gives access, than by the friendships between individual characters. *The Newcomes* and *Philip,* in particular, are punctuated by the narrator's elegiac paeans to the 'rough kindly communion' experienced in taverns, artist's studios, and student lodgings (*NC* 316). Fittingly, the name given by Thackeray to the tavern most often frequented by the bohemian society of both novels is 'the Haunt', for not only does it resonate as a generic emblem of all such places of male sociability, but it also signifies the extent to which the image of bohemia constructed in his fiction is always already shaped through memory. Not surprisingly, the name of this tavern turns out to be eerily prophetic of its function within the retrospective mode of Pen's narratives: 'the Haunt' is, almost literally, a haunting place, full of the ghosts of old comrades, whom the telling of the story has reawoken.

The experience of bohemia, then, is commonly treated as belonging to a vanished world of the past, both at the level of the narrator's (and protagonist's) personal growth into maturity and of the wider process of cultural and historical change registered by him. In *The Newcomes*, 'the Haunt' becomes synonymous with Pen's lost premarital self and with a lost pre-Victorian idyll, which, in terms of the novel's broader thematic concerns, instantiates a true 'society of gentlemen'. It is in both of these senses that the narrator laments the passing of 'the Haunt': 'It has vanished: it is to be found no more: neither by night nor by day – unless the ghosts of good fellows still haunt it' (*NC* 318). This elegiac invocation of bohemian society adumbrates the repressive nature of bourgeois familial and professional norms, whilst apparently accepting their inexorable cultural development. Similarly, the young Philip escapes from the stifling formality of Dr Firmin's genteel household into a bohemian utopia, 'a land where men call each other by their Christian names; where most are poor, where almost all are young, and where, if a few oldsters do enter, it is because they have preserved more tenderly and carefully than other folks their youthful spirits, and the delightful capacity to be idle' (*WMT* xi. 148). But, like his friend Pen, who complains of having 'lost my way to Bohemia now' (*WMT* xi. 148), and like Clive Newcome before him, Philip must ultimately learn to abandon idleness and adjust himself to the cold bourgeois imperative of labour. To this extent, Thackeray's bohemian writers and artists absorb a similar lesson to other heroes of the Victorian *Bildungsroman* (David Copperfield or Pip of *Great Expectations*, for example), albeit under duress. While it is possible to evade the disciplines of marital and professional responsibility for a time, in the end the external force of social respectability inevitably prevails.

It is in *Philip* that the pressure generated by this external coercion is most strongly felt and resisted. As John Peck has noted, Philip is a 'disturbingly anti-social hero, quite different from the maturing hero or heroine we encounter in many Victorian novels'.[9] His troubled masculinity, which rebels against the veneer of middle-class respectability, but is then forced to abandon a bohemian relaxation of social inhibitions, issues in sporadic outbursts of physical violence and uncontrollable rage, often manifested in terms of hatred for a racialized other. Far more than any other of Thackeray's young bohemians, Philip appears, at times, to be genuinely and dangerously cut adrift from the cultural and moral norms associated with his original class status; not merely, as in the case of Warrington and Pen, a gentleman whose temporary social degradation is an act of feigned classlessness. The atavistic aggression displayed by the hero of *Philip,* however, is duplicated at the level of Pen's narratorial commentary. Assuming that the preponderance of his readers is female, and thus averse to his penchant for recounting Philip's 'bachelor habits', Pen jokingly remarks that 'a novel must not smell of cigars much, nor should its refined and genteel page be stained with too frequent brandy-and-water' (*WMT* xi. 215). Given that *Philip* was originally serialized in the pages of the *Cornhill Magazine,* a periodical explicitly conceived by Thackeray as suitable for 'family' reading, this observation appears incongruous in the novel's immediate context of publication, but commensurate with its figuration of a type of exaggerated masculinity, which violently rejects the trammels of the 'refined and genteel'. At the same time, this coded address to the female readership of the *Cornhill Magazine is* emblematic of the ambiguous status of women within Thackeray's practice of domestic realism. Excluded from the male homosocial community of bohemia, women are, nevertheless, inscribed into the elaborate narrative structure of the Pendennis novels through the choric voice of Laura, Pen's spouse and domestic 'angel'. Thus, the position of women within the bourgeois family remains closely aligned to the narrative and ideological centre of these novels, but peripheral to their real focus of attention, which is on the relations between men. In this regard, as in others, Thackeray's appropriation of the domestic novel effects a compromise between the demands of family romance, conventionally gendered as a feminine form, and the desire to write a more truthful, 'masculine', type of fiction.

4

Historiography and Historical Fiction

Despite its absorption in the material particularities of early-to-mid nineteenth-century culture, Thackeray's realist fiction derives, in part, from a self-conscious affiliation to the literary traditions of the eighteenth century past, as I observed in the previous chapter. In many Victorian reviews, he was, indeed, depicted as the Fielding of the nineteenth century: an oxymoron that neatly encapsulates the sense of temporal dislocation, or anachronism, that characterizes his relation to the process of history in general. During the 1850s, Thackeray's fascination with the cultural past became more pronounced as he embarked on a career as a public lecturer, specializing in historical subjects drawn from the preceding century. A series of lectures on 'The English Humourists of the Eighteenth Century', his literary precursors in the field of satire and social comedy, was delivered in Britain and the United States in 1851–2, and the formula repeated, three years later, in *The Four Georges* (1855–7), a sequence comprising 'sketches of manners, morals, court, and town life' over more than a century of Hanoverian rule from the dynastic accession of 1714. In consequence of these lecture series, Thackeray was viewed by some contemporaries as a historian of considerable stature: on the death of Thomas Babington Macaulay, the most influential Whig historian of the period, he was invited to write a history of the reign of Queen Anne as a supplement to Macaulay's unfinished *History of England* (1848–61), a project in which he remained interested for the remainder of his life. More immediately, lecturing on the eighteenth century served as preparation for writing two novels that were of equal importance in cementing his reputation as an informed historian of the period: *The History of Henry Esmond* (1852) and *The Virginians* (1857–9). It is these texts that represent Thackeray's most considered contribution to the development of the 'historical novel', a distinct genre of Victorian fiction established by Walter Scott's 'Waverley' novels in the early part of the nineteenth century.

At one level, the detached eighteenth-century settings of *Henry Esmond* and *The Virginians* can, justifiably, be distinguished from the novels of more or less contemporary social manners written by Thackeray during the same decade. Yet it is also best to avoid treating the 'historical' fiction as a purely autonomous branch of his literary production, as if a concern with history were merely equivalent to the representation of the past. In the first place, Thackeray's use of eighteenth-century settings extends back to the very beginning of his novel-writing career: to his parodies of the Newgate novel in *Catherine* and *Barry Lyndon,* the latter of which was originally subtitled *A Romance of the Last Century.* Though not primarily conceived as a historical novel, in the mould established by Scott, *Barry Lyndon* bears important similarities to the narrative and historiographical principles embodied in *Henry Esmond.* Furthermore, even in those novels in which 'history' is not represented as a discrete period setting, a process of historical change and/or continuity is shown to connect the present moment of the Victorian text to its immediately preceding cultural past. Most notably, the narrative of *Vanity Fair* begins 'while the present century was in its teens' (*VF* 3), during the Regency of the future King George IV, and spans the following two decades, before ending in the incipient Victorian period of the 1830s. Thus, on the one hand, it can be read as an antiquarian reconstruction of a distinctively pre-Victorian cultural milieu, whilst, at the same time, the indeterminate demarcation between past and present disallows the Victorian reader a comforting innoculation from its satire. A similar, but less pronounced, effect can be observed within *Pendennis, The Newcomes,* and *Philip,* each of which stages a narrative of historical and cultural development, alongside one of individual growth, from the early to mid-nineteenth century, a span of time roughly corresponding to Thackeray's own adult experience. Almost all his novels, then, stretch expansively within the dimension of history and time, in stark contrast to their relatively narrow spatial and sociological range.

It is, nevertheless, true that Thackeray's historical interests lie almost exclusively within the recent past, unlike those of Scott and many of his other successors. Despite having, at one time, entertained the possibility of writing a historical romance set in the reign of Henry V, he generally eschewed the fashionable Victorian cult of Medievalism in favour of what is now often termed the 'long eighteenth century' – a period of history conceived as stretching continuously from the Glorious Revolution of the late seventeenth century through to the Regency of the early nineteenth century. Thackeray's concentrated fascination with this period lends not only an empirical depth of knowledge, but also a sense of narrative cohesion, to his historical writing. At the beginning of the first of his lectures on *The Four Georges*, for example, a revelation of historical continuity is glimpsed through a recollection of his personal acquaintance with an elderly woman, whose own personal associations reach back in time to the reign of Queen Anne:

> I often thought, as I took my kind old friend's hand, how with it I held on to the old society of wits and men of the world. I could travel back for sevenscore years of time – have glimpses of Brummel, Selwyn, Chesterfield, and the men of pleasure; of Walpole and Conway; of Johnson, Reynolds, Goldsmith; of North, Chatham, Newcastle; of the fair maids of honour of George IL's Court; of the German retainers of George I.'s; where Addison was Secretary of State; where Dick Steele held a place; whither the great Marlborough came with his fiery spouse; when Pope, and Swift, and Bolingbroke yet lived and wrote. (*WMT* vii. 621)

Here, the figure of the 'old friend' provides a concrete embodiment of the coalescence of individual and collective memory, which forms so distinctive a feature of Thackeray's historical imagination. Through the writer's contiguity with this figure, the past life of the eighteenth century is brought into intimate proximity with the Victorian present, whilst its aura of antiquity is simultaneously enhanced. This anecdote is characteristic of Thackeray's procedure in both his historical lectures and novels, inasmuch as it presents the past as the evolutionary pre-history of the present, rather than as its irretrievable other.

LET HISTORY RISE UP

In the opening chapter of *The History of Henry Esmond*, Thackeray, speaking in the character of its eponymous narrator, enunciates the principles according to which his historical narrative will be constructed. It is possible to claim that Thackeray speaks with his narrator in this instance (though it is by no means true of the novel as a whole), since the thoughts on 'History' expressed by Esmond are repeated, with striking consistency, in differing contexts, throughout Thackeray's career. As in the case of the classical 'Tragic Muse', Esmond reflects, the 'Muse of History' has traditionally 'encumbered herself with ceremony', speaking in solemn tones of the majesty of kings, 'waiting on them obsequiously and stately, as if she were but a mistress of Court ceremonies, and had nothing to do with the registering of the affairs of the common people' (*HE* 13). History, in its authorized accounts, is written not only 'from above', as is now commonly understood, but also from a distance, which maintains the semblance of dignity ascribed to its heroic protagonists. Seeking to disrupt this 'official' historiographical procedure, to puncture its majestic facade, Esmond presents a manifesto for an alternative historical method:

> Why shall History go on kneeling to the end of time? I am for having her rise up off her knees, and take a natural posture: not to be for ever performing cringes and congees like a Court-chamberlain, and shuffling backwards out of doors in the presence of the sovereign. In a word, I would have History familiar rather than heroic: and think that Mr Hogarth and Mr Fielding will give our children a much better idea of the manners of the present age in England, than the Court *Gazette* and the newspapers which we get thence. (*HE* 14)

The radical rhetoric of this manifesto is interesting for what it proclaims, even though it might be argued that Esmond's/Thackeray's historiographical practice in some ways fails to deliver. It suggests, first, that Esmond's narrative will pay equal or greater attention to the 'ordinary', everyday experience of 'common people' living within the past, than to the 'great' public figures and events of written history, and, secondly, that its treatment of the latter will eschew the servile reverence of the 'Court' historian. In both respects, History is to be made 'familiar rather than heroic' by approaching the life of the past from an intentionally myopic and microscopic viewpoint. The ideal of familiarity implies both the legitimacy of the private or domestic sphere as a subject of history and of a privatized perspective on reputedly heroic subjects. This alternative historical method is associated with satire, and with the work of the novelist in particular, as opposed to more 'factual' sources of knowledge.

Two examples of this satirical irreverence towards 'heroic' figures of History are provided in chapter I by Esmond's anecdotal descriptions of personal glimpses of King Louis XIV of France and Queen Anne. The former, while 'persisting in enacting through life the part of Herb', is, on close inspection, 'but a little wrinkled old man, pock-marked, and with a great periwig and red heels to make him look tall', and the latter 'a hot, red-faced woman, not in the least resembling that statue of her which turns it stone back upon St Paul's , and faces the coaches struggling up Ludgate Hill' (*HE* 13–14). Esmond's near-sighted perspective, which dwells on the grotesque particulars of the physical body, is thus contrasted with the various idealizing forms of cultural representation – public statuary, portraiture, and literary romance – that support the official version of History. This satirical technique suggests an awareness that what passes for historical truth is, in part, determined by the specific modes of representation that are deployed in order to produce it, rather than being a set of unalterable empirical facts. More specifically, however, it illustrates the truth of a dictum attributed to the French historian Michelet, which Thackeray never tired of quoting, that 'no man is a hero to his valet'. The figure of the valet, or in this instance King Louis's barber, embodies the intimate familiarity that corrodes the aura of the hero, whilst also conveying the democratic political resonance of History seen from 'below'. Thackeray's acquaintance with this dictum is most likely to derive from his reading of Carlyle, whose historical lectures on the subject of heroes and hero worship mount a sustained attack on the premiss behind it. For Carlyle, it is as much the fault of the 'valet' as it is the deficiency of the hero that the former is unable to recognize the latter: the prevalence of 'sham' heroes in modern society does not invalidate the capacity for heroism *per se*.[1] In a review of Carlyle's *French Revolution* (1837), Thackeray professed sympathy for this viewpoint, arguing that 'it is better to view .. . [the Revolution] loftily from afar, like our mystic poetic Mr Carlyle, than too nearly with sharp-sighted and prosaic Thiers'. The French historian, he declares, is 'the *valet de chambre* of this history, he is too familiar with its dishabille and off-scourings: it can never be a hero to him' (*WMT* xiii. 240). Yet, despite his early appreciation of Carlyle, Thackeray came increasingly to identify his own historiographical posture with the despised figure of the *valet de chambre* , thus effectively retracting the preference expressed in this review. By the time of *The Four Georges*, the conceptual opposition between 'lofty' and 'sharp-sighted' historical methods remains unchanged, but his allegiance has clearly switched sides. Distinguishing between 'history – of which I do not aspire to be an expounder – and manners and life such as these sketches would describe' (*WMT* vii. 638), Thackeray outlines the perspective from which he observes the 'historical' event of the Duke of Marlborough returning to London from exile on the death of Queen Anne:

> We are with the mob in the crowd, not with the great folks in the procession. We are not the Historic Muse, but her Ladyship's attendant, tale-bearer – *valet de chambre* – for whom no man is a hero; and, as yonder one steps from his carriage to the next handy conveyance, we take the number of the hack; we look all over at his stars, ribands, embroidery; we think within ourselves, O you unfathomable schemer! (*WMT* vii. 639)

The subversive implication of identification with the figure of the valet is apparent from this resonant political image of the historian witnessing the procession of 'great folks' from his place 'with the mob'. How seriously this rhetoric of subversion can be taken, however, remains a moot point. A less sympathetic interpretation of his statements might suggest that

Thackeray is merely offering his support for a self-consciously trivial version of history – one that shies away from the analysis of public political events in favour of an impressionistic observation of 'manners and life'.

In his classic study *The Historical Novel*, the Marxist critic Georg Lukács makes precisely this criticism of Thackeray, arguing that the apparent radicalism of his anti-heroic historiography leads to an essentially private and subjectivist conception of history, one that reduces the discussion of politics to the level of gossip.[2] Thackeray's irreverent characterization of Marlborough as an 'unfathomable schemer' in *The Four Georges is*, indeed, carried over into his fictional representation of Esmond's personal animus against the Duke, suggesting one of numerous autobiographical projections within *Henry Esmond*. But, as Lukács himself acknowledges, the arbitrarily subjective basis of Esmond's hostility to Marlborough is itself thematized within both the form and the content of the novel. Esmond's autobiographical narrative, though written predominantly in the third person, does not attempt to disguise its lack of impartiality in judging the people and events that come within the narrator's experience – a characteristic that is further emphasized by the fictitious editorial apparatus of the 'Preface' and occasional footnotes, wherein Rachel Esmond Warrington, Henry's daughter, draws attention to her father's idiosyncracies (a device similar to that employed in the original version of *Barry Lyndon*). Esmond even goes to the extent of forewarning his descendants of the danger of accepting the truth of his portrait of Marlborough, as 'very likely a private pique of his own may be the cause of his ill-feeling' (*HE* 243). In this manner, his narrative exposes the way in which our cultural recollection of 'great' historical figures is filtered through differential codes of literary representation, which are themselves contingent upon the vagaries of subjective experience. Had Marlborough shown a 'word of kindness or acknowledgement, or a single glance of approbation' towards him, the narrator suggests, it 'might have changed Esmond's opinion of the great man; and instead of a satire, which his pen cannot help writing, who knows but that the humble historian might have taken the other side of panegyric? We have but to change the point of view, and the greatest action looks mean; as we turn the perspective-glass, and a giant appears a pigmy' (*HE* 244). Lukács is right to infer that this insistence upon the irreducibly private motivation behind acts of ideological commitment that shape the representation of historical figures, and even alter the course of historical events, leads, ultimately, to a conception of history as determined by chance, according to the arbitrary needs and desires of disassociated individuals. By making the randomness of Esmond's experience so transparent, however, Thackeray signals the limitations of his individual perspective, while arguing for the inadequacy of those rationalist accounts of history that tend to downplay the importance of subjectivity.

Thackeray's critique of Carlylean historiography is also less consistent or straightforward than is often assumed. While Esmond adopts a subversive, valet's-eye view of Marlborough and the Old Pretender, revealing the petty human frailties that, in his experience, underlie their heroic facades, he is remarkably uncritical and sentimental, for example, in his reflections on King William, to whose political cause he retrospectively converts, calling him 'the greatest, the wisest, the bravest, and most clement sovereign whom England ever knew' (*HE* 188). This apparent discrepancy in his attitude towards the heroic is, in fact, characteristic of the underlying narrative movement of *Henry Esmond*, which repeatedly, and in parallel sequence, traces the development, disenchantment, and reconstitution of quasi-religious forms of worship. Esmond is as much the deluded victim of this process as its cynical observer, in terms of both his sexual and his political allegiances. If the great epiphanic climax of the novel is reached at the moment when Esmond simultaneously recognizes and renounces the folly of his worship of Beatrix and the Stuart cause, his habitual tendency to seek idealized objects of love and belief continues afterwards in less obtrusive forms. Just as King William supplants the Old Pretender in Esmond's political credo, so, to some extent, Rachel takes the place of Beatrix as the idol of his sexual needs, as the endemic religious vocabulary surrounding her suggests. Although the retrospective narrative mode implies that the elderly Esmond, recounting his now distant youthful indiscretions from a position of clear-sighted maturity, is free from the dangers of such misguided worship, the effect of these substitutions is merely concealed. Moreover, Esmond himself is treated as an object of blind devotion both within his narrative, by Rachel, and outside it, in his daughter's hagiographical Preface. Thackeray's ironic insinuation is that the lesson of Esmond's experience has not been learned, by either himself, his eventual wife, or the future recipient of his tale, in spite of all the narrator's claims to demystify the false illusions of his age. The idealist historiography, which both Thackeray and Esmond attempt to undermine, remains stubbornly persistent, as *The Virginians, a* loosely conceived sequel to *Henry Esmond,* also appears to conclude. In this later novel, the patently idealized figures of George Washington and James Wolfe suggest a strange determination, on Thackeray's part, to demonstrate that he is capable of balancing the panegyric mode against the satirical in his representation of historical 'heroes'.

What is arguably a more radical innovation in Thackeray's historiography is his application of the, perspective of the valet to the defining events of history, as distinct from its protagonists. From *Barry Lyndon* through to *Vanity Fair, Henry Esmond,* and *The Virginians,* a recurring feature of his historical fiction is its terse, unsentimentalized hostility towards the glorification of war. In the first of these novels, the narrator's experience of the battle of Minden, during the Seven Years War, is recalled with a mixture of explicit disdain for the distorting sensationalism of conventional 'romance-writers' and half-conscious revelry in the brutality that he claims to decry. The black comedy of Barry's vacillation between military *braggodocio* and humanitarian concern does not conceal the serious purpose with which the scene is described. Professing to speak only from 'my own personal experience', Barry is forced to acknowledge his peripheral participation in an 'event' that appears to have taken place some 'two miles off', and that 'none of us soldiers of the line knew of what had occurred until we came to talk about the fight over our kettles in the evening, and repose after the labours of a hard-fought day' (*BL* 69–70). Thus, as in the more famous lacuna at the centre of Thackeray's account of the battle of Waterloo in *Vanity Fair,* History occurs somewhere else, aside from the experience of the ordinary foot-soldier, and can be compreh ended, in narrative terms, only after the fact. All that remains of Barry's first-hand experience of the battle is a series of disconnected sensory impressions recalling his savage killing of a 'poor little ensign':

> The ensign's silver *bellboy* box and his purse of gold; the livid face of the poor fellow as he fell; the huzzas of the men of my company as I went out under a smart fire and rifled him; their shouts and curses as we came hand in hand with the Frenchmen – these are, in truth, not very dignified recollections, and had best be passed over briefly. (*BL* 70–1)

The satirical force of this episode derives from its juxtaposition of two separate and competing claims to historical knowledge. Although Barry cannot truthfully claim to have been 'present' at what is retrospectively construed as the battle of Minden, his limited and inferior perspective reveals more about the orchestrated chaos of war than any dispassionate history of the event. The undignified character of his recollections is, of course, their point, designed to shatter the spurious dignity with which the 'Historical Muse' recounts her tales of military glory. As Barry laconically remarks: 'If people would tell their stories of battles in this simple way, I think the cause of truth would not suffer by it' (*BL* 70).

Henry Esmond is, in some ways, an opposing figure to Barry Lyndon in relation to their common role as observers of the realities of war. Whereas Barry's avowed humility is always straining to suppress a comically inflated sense of his martial prowess, Esmond's account of his 'life of action' in Marlborough's army is less ironically intended to underplay the extent of his 'military exploits', despite the fact that it takes up roughly a third of the whole novel (*HE* 199–200). Yet the critical content of Thackeray's representation of their experience of war is essentially the same. As in the earlier novel, the narrator is at pains to show the reader aspects of military life that the 'stately Muse of History, that delights in describing the valour of heroes and the grandeur of conquest' tends to 'leave out': the 'burning farms, wasted fields, shrieking women, slaughtered sons and fathers, and drunken soldiery, cursing and carousing in the midst of tears, terror, and murder' (*HE* 235). Similarly, Esmond's participation in the celebrated battle of Blenheim is both marginal and singularly unheroic, for 'almost at the very commencement of this famous day . . . a shot brought down his horse and our young gentleman on it, who fell crushed and stunned under the animal; and came to his senses he knows not how long after, only to lose them again from pain and loss of blood' (*HE* 238–9). Like Barry, in other words, he views History taking place from close quarters, and discovers only a bathetic absence of meaning at its core. The implicit contrast between Esmond's subjective experience of war and the manner in which history is constructed from a distance is reinforced when he subsequently encounters Joseph Addison in the process of composing *The Campaign* (1703), his triumphal poem on the victory of Blenheim. The ensuing debate between the two men goes to the heart of the aesthetic and historiographical principles embodied within *Henry Esmond*. For Esmond, Addison's poetic representation of the historical event that he has just 'experienced' is no more than 'murder . . . done to military music':

> You hew out of your polished verses a stately image of smiling victory; *I* tell you 'tis an uncouth, distorted, savage idol; hideous, bloody, and barbarous. The rites performed before it are shocking to think of. You great poets should show it as it is – ugly and horrible, not beautiful and serene. Oh, sir, had you made the campaign, believe me, you never would have sung it so. (*HE* 254–5)

Addison, however, remains perfectly conscious of the aestheticization of historical reality performed by his poem: it is the consequence of his decision to write in a style that is 'harmonious and majestic, not familiar, or too near the vulgar truth' (*HE* 255–6). This aesthetic validation of the style of *The Campaign* is, arguably, defensible, but it becomes discredited when Addison's collusion with the transparently ideological arena of political patronage is revealed. As Esmond notes, *The Campaign* is not merely an idealized aesthetic representation of military heroism, but, more specifically, Whig propaganda on behalf of Marlborough, which serves the material self-interest of both poet and subject alike. Thus, this debate recapitulates Esmond's distinction between 'heroic' and 'familiar' History in chapter I, and Thackeray leaves the reader in little doubt as to whose representation of the historical event comes closer to the truth.

PROGRESS AND REPETITION

Thackeray's choice of subject for *Henry Esmond* was a bold one, given its proximity to that of Scott's *Waverley* (1814), the first and most influential of all nineteenth-century historical novels. By setting the action of his own historical fiction within the period ranging, approximately, from the Glorious Revolution of 1688 through to the Hanoverian succession of 1714, Thackeray invites comparison with Scott's treatment of the Jacobite rebellion of 1745, an event that emerged directly out of the preceding half-century of political and religious conflict between Tories and Whigs, Protestants and Catholics, Stuarts and Hanoverians. In a sense, Thackeray's text would seem to offer a pre-history of the foundational moment of the historical novel, an interpretation that can be traced through various coded allusions to its predecessor. Most notably, *Henry Esmond* echoes *Waverley* in employing as its protagonist, and focal consciousness, a man whose 'wavering' allegiance to both sides of the political divide enables him to embody the broader historical crisis that the novel seeks to explore. Like Edward Waverley, Esmond is raised in a family that holds strong sympathies for the deposed Stuart dynasty, and its associated Roman Catholicism, and becomes embroiled in conspiring for its restoration, whilst, both retrospectively and at the same time, questioning the validity of his commitment. Just as Waverley is ultimately reconciled with the Hanoverian political establishment, so Esmond eventually renounces the Stuart Pretender and recounts the story of his youthful Toryism from the perspective of an elderly Whig. By following the narrative of *Waverley* so closely, Thackeray signals a similar examination of ideological ambivalence, of conservative attraction to the glamour of the Legitimist cause and progressivist acceptance of the new social order, but appears more determined than Scott to demolish the romantic allure of the former. The debauched cynicism of the 'Old Pretender' (James Edward Stuart) in *Henry Esmond*, for instance, can be read as a critique of the charismatic idealism of the 'Young Pretender' (Charles Edward Stuart) in *Waverley*. At the level of conscious political argument, Thackeray lends clearer support to the Whig notion of beneficent historical progess than does the conservatively inclined Scott – a shift that some critics have attributed to the intervening influence of Macaulay.[3]

The 'progressive' aspect of the historical narrative inscribed within *Henry Esmond*, however, is not so much a product of Esmond's formal political conversion, which, in any case, remains less than unambiguous, than it is a matter of his instinctive attunement to the emergence of what is perceived to be a new cultural sensibility. Even during his most fervent period of Tory loyalism, Esmond readily concedes that the Whigs have better manners. His preference for the Whig propagandists Steele and, to a lesser extent, Addison over the Tory Swift is presented as symptomatic of his affinity with a code of gentlemanliness that privileges the incipient bourgeois virtues of domesticity and respect for women over a rakish aristocratic culture of misogyny. It is, thus, appropriate that the immediate cause of Esmond's renunciation of the Stuart claim is his revulsion at the act of sexual indiscretion committed jointly by the Old Pretender and his cousin Beatrix – conflict within the arena of high politics is symbolically connected to a more deep-seated cultural division, in which sexual morality and the politics of gender are the real issues at stake. As has often been noted, Esmond's dualistic representation of Rachel and Beatrix as 'virgin' and 'whore' encodes a cultural sensibility that is not so much covertly Whiggish as proto-Victorian. In schematic opposition to her daughter's role as *femme fatale*, Rachel is repeatedly ascribed the characteristics of the Victorian bourgeois ideal of domestic femininity, the figure of the 'angel in the house' whose 'virtue is like that of a saint in heaven' (*HE* 187). In this light, Thackeray's historiographical postulation of a conflict of sexual manners within the early eighteenth century seems patently anachronistic. The substitution of Rachel for Beatrix as Esmond's feminine ideal at the culmination of the narrative dramatizes a cultural shift that goes well beyond the temporal boundaries of the novel's fictive historical setting. Commenting on this narrative trajectory, Eve Kosofsky Sedgwick has observed how 'a family that begins as rakish, reactionary, Catholic, Jacobite aristocracy ... turns within a few years to a piously Protestant, Whiggish, obsessionally domestic home circle of, essentially, solid mid-Victorian citizens'.[4] A similar example of the coalescence of linear narrative development and historical progression can be located in *The Virginians*. The bizarrely disjointed structure of this novel, in which the tale of Harry Warrington's picaresque adventures in the corrupt, hedonistic world of mid-eighteenth-century English society is abruptly succeeded by George Warrington's introverted autobiographical memoir, can be seen as enacting a generic shift from eighteenth- to nineteeth-century narrative modes.

In neither of these texts, however, does the historical progression performed by the narrative amount to an unequivocal endorsement of the Whig ideology of Progress. The irony of Esmond's dualistic configuration of Rachel and Beatrix, for example, is that, whereas the logic of historical development would suggest that one outmoded cultural construction of femininity (the aristocratic *femme fatale)* is to be replaced by another (the bourgeois domestic 'angel'), the logic of genealogy – the biological succession from mother to daughter – suggests a different narrative sequence. As Sedgwick points out, Beatrix's aristocratic eighteenth-century typology of femininity is, in fact, presented as a *product* of Rachel's oppressively bourgeois, 'Victorian' domestic virtue – as, precisely, a reaction against it.[5] In a similar vein, the corrupted sexuality of Rachel's daughter refers back to that of the first Viscountess of Castlewood, herself a mistress of Stuart royalty, whom the virtuous Rachel has symbolically displaced, thus further blurring the prospect of linear cultural development. If Esmond and Rachel are taken to embody idealized types of masculine and feminine virtue, both belonging to the historical future evoked by the novel's narrative trajectory, the future is not presented as uniformly bright. The figure of Beatrix functions as a dissenting satirical voice, which calls into question the cultural values that they anticipate. Hence, Esmond's moral earnestness and melancholic introspection, which have led some critics to complain of Thackeray's apparent endorsement of 'Victorian respectability',[6] is already subjected to an ironic, 'eighteenth-century' interrogation within the text.

In *The Virginians,* Thackeray develops a cruder, more explicit mechanism for questioning the assumption of moral progress that underpins the nineteenth-century novelist's representation of the eighteenth-century past. Echoing the subtitle of Scott's *Waverley: or, 'Tis Sixty Years Since,* the novel is punctuated by open reminders of the period of 100 years that separates the omniscient narrator's composition of the text from its historical setting. This constant comparison between past and present serves as a way of distancing readers from the fictive world of the text, and refocusing attention onto the cultural expectations that they themselves bring to it. While the narrator superficially flatters the Victorian reader's consciousness of moral superiority over the corrupt eighteenth century, in reality his intention is to satirize such complacency. The following passage is one of numerous examples of this technique: 'A hundred years ago people of the great world were not so straitlaced as they are now, when everybody is good, pure, moral, modest; when there is no skeleton in anybody's closet; when there is no scheming; no slurring over of old stories; when no girl tries to sell herself for wealth, and no mother abets her' (*WMT* x. 145). It is clear that the narrator gives little credence to the dominant self-conception of the Victorian age of moral improvement, to which he is, nevertheless, obliged to pay lip-service. The confusion of moral virtue with a 'squeamish' refusal to discuss subjects that were openly available to the eighteenth-century novelist of manners provides a constant source of irritation to the would-be historical novelist of the nineteenth century. At best, Thackeray's handling of the transition from the aristocratic worldliness of the past to the purified bourgeois present is ambivalent: 'That old world was more dissolute than ours', the narrator concedes, but 'the frankness which characterized those easy times' exempts them from the charge of hypocrisy that he levels against the modern world (*WMT* x. 234, 319). In its most negative form, his comparison between the two periods deploys the eighteenth century primarily as a vehicle for critique of the nineteenth. Indeed, for a historical novel, *The Virginians is* remarkable for its narrator's frank acknowledgement of an inability to write in the authentic spirit of the past that he seeks to emulate. The result is not so much a full-bodied historicist reconstruction or simulation of the past, like that attempted in *Henry Esmond*, as a text that exposes the historical difference that prevents it from transcending the constricting horizons of the present.

More fundamentally, perhaps, the idea of history as meaningful progression is undermined by Thackeray's characteristic emphasis upon cyclical patterns of historical repetition, as well as on the mere random accumulation of events in time. Henry Esmond, as I have already noted, attributes his participation in the momentous ideological conflicts of his age to the arbitrary circumstances of his private experience. His conversion from Catholicism to the Anglican Church, his loyalty to the Jacobite cause, his pursuit of military fame under Marlborough, are all 'explained' by the unfathomable psychology of his love for Rachel and Beatrix: 'with people that take a side in politics', he declares, "tis men rather than principles that commonly bind them' (*HE* 372). In this respect, Esmond's career is shaped in parallel to that of the Old Pretender, whose condition of deposed legitimacy he obviously shares. At the dramatic climax of the novel, the reader is shown how the grand political events of history are, in part, determined by absurd accidents of personal character – by the Pretender's inability to control his momentary sexual predilection for Beatrix. A sense of the groundless contingency of historical process, rather than of any deep-rooted causality, hovers over this account of the defining moments of the Hanoverian succession. Moreover, just as Thackeray is conscious of the fact that the apparently conclusive events of 1714 will be replayed in the Jacobite rebellion of 1745, so the former is itself figured as a repetition of earlier abortive conspiracies adumbrated within the novel. Esmond's role in the plot to restore James Edward Stuart to the throne echoes the equally futile endeavours of both his real and surrogate fathers, extending back to the reign of William of Orange. The image of history fashioned in *Henry Esmond* thus reflects an experience of interminable and inexplicable repetition, yet one that is embodied in a surprisingly taut, and meaningful, dramatic form. Though emphasizing the irrational private sources of political struggle, as Lukács complains, Thackeray gives artistic shape to this otherwise arbitrary conception of history through an intricate series of analogies between the private and public spheres. The 'personal' narrative of Esmond's discovery and noble renunciation of his legitimate claim to the title of Marquis, and status as head of the Esmond family, can be read as an allegory of the struggle for legitimacy within the political narrative, the two spheres ultimately coalescing in the pivotal historical moment of 'August 1, 1714', the title of the novel's final chapter.

This dramatically cohesive presentation of the contingent experience of history is notably absent from the sequel to *Henry Esmond*. As Jack Rawlins has suggested, *The Virginians* can itself be viewed as a repetition of *Henry Esmond*, but one that is composed in a very different narrative style.[7] While the novel traces the history of a succeeding generation of the Esmond family, in which familiar figures, such as an elderly Beatrix, reappear, its form more closely resembles the loose, digressive character of Thackeray's intervening work of fiction, *The Newcomes*. Thus, the recurrence of characters and motifs from *Henry Esmond* has the possibly intended effect of dissipating the narrative tension with which they have previously been invested, or even of dispelling their lingering romantic aura. Ironically, *The Virginians* appears to bear the same relationship to its predecessor as Esmond claimed for his response to conventional 'heroic' historiography. Thackeray's subtle treatment of the question of Esmond's love for an older woman, for example, is reduced to a subject of ribaldry in the later novel. In her grotesque reincarnation as the decrepit Baroness Bernstein, Beatrix's infatuation with the young Harry Warrington presents a tawdry echo of the relationship between his grandfather and her mother, as does the Oedipal triangulation of love and loathing between George Warrington, his mother Rachel Esmond Warrington, and his suspiciously homonymic rival for her affection, George Washington. The reader is made fully aware of this network of family resemblances, and is further encouraged to treat it as an object of low comedy when Harry becomes besotted with Lady Maria, a woman of middle age fully equipped with false teeth and hair. This irreverent, demystifying approach to a type of love that is celebrated as the culminating experience of Esmond's pursuit of happiness in the closing pages of *Henry Esmond is* symptomatic of the way in which history repeats itself in parodic form in *The Virginians*. The reappearance of Beatrix, cruelly transformed from her earlier status as the manifestation of desirable youth into a 'shrivelled old woman', provides an iconic focus for this strategy (*WMT* x. 708). What has happened to Beatrix in the interim between the two novels is nothing other than a result of the sheer passage of time, a process of ageing that implies no corresponding moral growth, as the narrator sententiously observes:

> All beauty must at last come to this complexion; and decay either under ground or on the tree. Here was old age, I fear, without reverence. Here were grey hairs, that were hidden, or painted. The world was still here, and she tottering on it, and clinging to it with her crutch. For fourscore years she had moved on it, and eaten of the tree, forbidden and permitted. (*WMT* x. 708)

From *Henry Esmond* to *The Virginians*, in other words, time has moved on, but in the same path as before, and without any meaningful purpose. The decay of beauty is one of the timeless effects of time, a static or circular event, which lends itself to Thackeray's characteristically baroque allegorical treatment. Similarly, in the more 'historical' sections of *The Virginians*, George Warrington's account of the War of American Independence bears an uncanny resemblance to his grandfather's experience of political conflict in the earlier novel. Like Esmond, George fights on the side of 'Tory' loyalism, this time attempting to preserve the legitimate sovereignty of the Hanoverian George III, whilst secretly sympathizing with the 'Whig' cause of rebellion. The terms of the struggle are, on the one hand, ironically inverted, but, on the other, precisely the same. Beneath the superficial differences of costume and setting, Thackeray presents the later event as a re-enactment of the former, which, in its turn, was only the latest in a sequence of seemingly inconclusive historical repetitions.

MEMORIES FROM THE END OF TIME

Perhaps the most distinctive aspect of Thackeray's contribution to the development of the nineteenth-century historical novel, however, is the importance that he attaches to the faculty of memory. In each of his later historical fictions – *Henry Esmond, The Virginians*, and the unfinished *Denis Duval* (posthumously published in 1864) – it is the vitality of the subjective memory of the narrating consciousness that enriches the otherwise potentially arid antiquarian exploration of the past. In the first and last-mentioned of these texts, this memory belongs avowedly to a fictive autobiographical persona, whereas in *The Virginians*, as elsewhere in Thackeray's fiction, it issues more directly from the consciousness of the author. Yet the memory of the narrator, particularly when it can be assumed to correspond to that of the real author, often seeks to stimulate an act of shared cultural memory with the assumed contemporary reader, broadening its scope beyond individual reminiscence. One of the more striking effects of Thackeray's predilection for writing about the relatively recent historical past is the ease with which it allows him to align the trajectories of objective and subjective time – the grand historical figures and events of the eighteenth century and the quasi-living memory of the nineteenth.

The narratorial posture that Thackeray adopts in order to reinforce this illusion of unity between history and memory is that of the self-confessed 'old fogey', the man of mature experience who looks back on the more adventurous time of his youth as on a period of ancient history. Henry Esmond, as I have observed, writes his narrative in a time and a place far removed from that of the principal events that it recounts. Hence, as Andrew Sanders points out, Esmond's 'history is an act of memory', simultaneously bridging and widening the gulf between past and present.[8] Writing in connection to one of the many traumatic memories of his past life, the doubleness of this temporal perspective becomes apparent: 'He is old now who recalls you. Long ago he has forgiven and blest the soft hand that wounded him: but the mark is there, and the wound is cicatrized only – no time, tears, caresses, or repentance, can obliterate the scar' (*HE* 173). On the one hand, the distancing of the experience of his past to a time that, at the moment of writing, seems 'long ago' aligns Esmond's narratorial viewpoint with that of the contemporary (Victorian) reader of the text, while, on the other, the capacity of memory to preserve the 'scar' of the past brings the reader closer to the time of 'history'. Similarly, when George Warrington assumes the narration of the last third of *The Virginians*, it is in the guise of an avuncular 'elderly gentleman', recalling the trials of his early married life and his experience of the War of American Independence, whilst 'sitting in my comfortable easy-chair' (*WMT* x. 690). Even in the case of *Denis Duval*, a historical romance written in the mould of Alexandre Dumas, and with the avowed intention of purging the relaxed digressive style of his later fiction, Thackeray opts for a retrospective first-person narrative, written some fifty years after the events of the story have elapsed, when 'the curtain is down, and the play long over' (*WMT* xii. 469). Indeed, to an even greater extent than its predecessors, *Denis Duval* insists upon a radical temporal disjunction between the originary moment of experience and the secondary moment of writing, the latter being equated with the reminiscential habit of old age:

> Why do I make zig-zag journeys? 'Tis the privilege of old age to be garrulous, and its happiness to remember early days. As I sink back in my arm-chair, safe and sheltered post *tot discriniina,* and happier than it has been the lot of most fellow-sinners to be, the past comes back to me – the stormy past, the strange unhappy yet happy past – and I look at it scared and astonished sometimes; as huntsmen look at the gaps and ditches over which they have leapt, and wonder how they are alive. (*WMT* xii. 490–1)

The figure of the 'arm-chair' narrator, safely ensconced in the domestic idyll of old age, is thus common to almost all Thackeray's historical novels; only the elderly Barry Lyndon, who writes his memoirs from the discomfort of a prison cell, provides a partial exception to the type. Situated at the end of his life, and seemingly at the end of time itself, the consciousness of this narratorial figure is nothing other than the sum total of his memories, through which he is free to roam discontinuously, or on 'zig-zag journeys' between past, present, and future. As J. Hillis Miller observes in relation to *Henry Esmond,* it is as if the narrator thereby assumes the capacity of 'total memory', recollecting his life from the perspective of someone who is already dead.

As Hillis Miller points out, the most important cultural source of Thackeray's construction of narratorial memory can be found in Wordsworth's famous definition of poetry as a form of 'emotion recollected in tranquillity', outlined in his preface to the second edition of *Lyrical Ballads* (1800).[10] The temporal and temperamental standpoint of Thackeray's narrators, most notably Esmond and Duval, strongly resembles that of a Wordsworthian poetics of memory, as does Thackeray's conceptualization of the workings of memory throughout their texts. The broadly linear, sequential unfolding of Esmond's autobiographical narrative, for instance, is punctuated by a series of intense moments of experience, which seem to defy any attempt at a merely chronological ordering of time. Esmond retrospectively picks out those moments of his past experience that have since become indelibly imprinted upon his memory, but, paradoxically, appears to do so at the very moment of their occurrence, before the memories have had time, chronologically, to form. The memory of being ordered to leave Castlewood (his adopted family home) by Rachel offers one example of this disruption of linear time:

> Esmond stood by the fireplace, blankly staring after her. Indeed, he scarce seemed to see until she was gone; and then her image was impressed upon him, and remained for ever fixed upon his memory. He saw her retreating, the taper lighting up her marble face, her scarlet lip quivering, and her shining golden hair. He went to his own room, and to bed, where he tried to read, as his custom was; but he never knew what he was reading until afterwards he remembered the appearance of the letters of the book (it was in Montaigne's Essays), and the events of the day passed before him – that is, of the last hour of the day; for as for the morning, and the poor milkmaid yonder, he never so much as once thought. (*HE* 87)

What is, perhaps, most striking about this recollection is its associative attachment to a particular visual scene or image (the figure of Rachel holding the taper) that is capable of acquiring secondary associations by contiguity with other objects (the volume of Montaigne's *Essays*). This complex accumulation of multiple strands of memory around a singular 'moment' of experience is reminiscent of the Wordsworthian conception of the 'spots of time' that reverberate throughout the chronological existence of the self, both shaping and disrupting the form of autobiographical narrative.[11] Needless to say, the attribution of a distinctly post-Romantic awareness of the associative power of memory to the consciousness of an early-eighteenth-century memoirist is, again, anachronistic. Esmond is distanced from the eighteenth century not only by the mere fact of his elderly, reminiscential perspective, but by the very form of his memory, which belongs, in fictive terms, to the future. The synthesis between this Wordsworthian practice of poetic recollection and the politicized historical romance of Scott is, arguably, the most innovative historiographical feature of *Henry Esmond*.

Yet Thackeray's intense preoccupation with memory, and the subjective apprehension of time, extends beyond the narrative demands of historical fiction to inform almost all his later writings. In *The Roundabout Papers* (1860–3), he conducts a sustained exercise in autobiographical retrospection, conceived under the more directly authorial guise of the editor of the *Cornhill Magazine*. Many of the essays in this series explore memories of youth, in which the cultural nostalgia of middle age is simultaneously celebrated and subverted. In 'De juventute' (a Latin word meaning 'youth'), for example, Thackeray reveals an awareness of the potentially self-deceptive character of memory that risks turning him into 'your mere twaddling *laudator ternporis acti – your* old fogey who can see no good except in his own time' (*WMT* xii. 236), but, nonetheless, revels in its imaginative satisfactions. Though the act of retrospection may distort a 'historical' apprehension of the past, its capacity to suspend the empirical reality of the present moment allows access to a parallel, but heightened, intensity of experience. Echoing Wordsworth once again, in 'Notes of a Week's Holiday', he conceives of the power of memory as a state of split-consciousness, in which a 'man can be alive in 1860 and 1830 at the same time': while the body lies 'inert, silent, torpid' in the present, the 'spirit' is able to inhabit the past, thus reawakening an earlier consciousness of presence (*WMT* xii. *244)*. Characteristically, Thackeray's memorial 'spirit' gives a decidedly material incarnation to Wordsworth's transcendent faculty: 'I am walking about in *1828*', he remembers, 'in a blue dress-coat and brass buttons, a sweet figured silk waistcoat (which I button round a slim waist with perfect ease), looking at beautiful beings with gigot sleeves and tea-tray hats under the golden chestnuts of the Tuileries' (*WMT* xii. 244). Here, as elsewhere in *The Roundabout Papers*, it is the ephemeral sensory experience of a seemingly banal material culture that provides the focus for nostalgic reminiscence. The meaning of these impressions derives purely from the specificity with which they are recollected, rather than from any 'higher', symbolic register. In 'Tunbridge Toys', for instance, Thackeray embarks upon a reminiscence of childhood by 'wonder[ing] whether those little silver pencil-cases with a movable almanack at the butt-end are still favourite implements with boys', before proceeding to itemize the miscellaneous contents of a schoolboy's pocket from personal memory (*WMT* xii. 223). The microscopically observed detail of the 'little silver pencil-case' functions as a sensory stimulus to memory, opening up a chain of associative recollections in a manner resembling Proust as much as Wordsworth. Later in the same essay, the memory of a childhood visit to a coffee shop is recalled with something of the visceral immediacy of the former: 'I remember the taste of the coffee and toast to this day – a peculiar, muddy, not-sweetenough, most fragrant coffee – a rich, rancid, yet-not-butteredenough, delicious toast' (*WMT* xii. 226).

According to John Carey, Thackeray's exploration of the effects of temporal dislocation produced by memory should not be confused with the programmatic modernist deconstruction of linear time, which it appears to anticipate. But, while this qualification is necessary, Carey's assertion that the preoccupation with the past in Thackeray's later writings is essentially escapist and consolatory in character seems equally questionable.[12] It would be more accurate to conclude that the reminiscential stance adopted in *The Roundabout Papers* and the later novels dramatizes an ambivalent consciousness of time, recognizing the sense of both loss and consolation inherent in the exercise of memory. This ambivalence is implied in the metaphor with which he chooses to characterize the nostalgic vision of the 'old fogey' at the beginning of 'On a Joke I Once Heard from the Late Thomas Hood':

> The good-natured reader who has perused some of these rambling papers has long since seen . . . that the writer belongs to the

> old-fashioned classes of this world, loves to remember very much more than to prophesy, and though he can't help being carried onward, and downward, perhaps, on the hill of life, the swift milestones marking their forties, fifties – how many tens or lustres shall we say? – he sits under Time, the white-wigged charioteer, with his back to the horses, and his face to the past, looking at the receding landscape and the hills fading into the grey distance. (*WMT* xii. 261)

Preferring to 'remember very much more than to prophesy', the later (or older) Thackeray acknowledges an inclination to live, comfortingly, in the past, averting his gaze from the present and future as he sits looking backwards from the chariot of Time. The 'rambling', circuitous structure of the anecdotes that comprise *The Roundabout Papers is* itself a manifestation of this desire to defer the progressive, linear onset of time. But this desire is tinged with frustration, as the 'receding landscape' of the past fades into the 'grey distance': memory is both stimulated and eroded by the passage of time. Thackeray is well aware that time cannot, ultimately, be deflected from its inexorable movement into the future, and he mourns the irretrievable passing of the past, as much as he finds consolation through it. As in Walter Benjamin's celebrated interpretation of Paul Klee's painting of *Angelus novus* – the 'angel of history' whose 'face is turned toward the past' as a storm from Paradise 'irresistibly propels him into the future' – Thackeray's metaphor of sitting 'under Time, the white-wigged charioteer' defines a perspective that is sensitively attuned to the cultural 'debris' left gathering in the wake of historical 'progress', though without manifesting any of the revolutionary-messianic hope of redemption from time that animates Benjamin's theory of history.[13]

In Thackeray, as I have suggested, the debris of history belongs, more often than not, to the obsolescent material fabric of a culture in which the process of change is not merely hastened, but governed at its deepest level, by the onset of modernity. Well before his writings of the late 1850s and 1860s, Thackeray's memory habitually dwells upon impressions of the clothes, coins, food, and artefacts that in the space of no more than thirty years have receded into a seemingly ancient past. The acute consciousness of temporal flux – or 'feeling of rapid transience', to use Carey's phrase[14] – that permeates both his fictional and non-fictional writings alike reflects an experience of history analagous to the logic of fashion, in which innovation and obsolescence are rapidly and ceaselessly interchanged. This experience of history can be linked, on the one hand, to the ideology of material progress that fuelled the self-proclaimed modernity of the Victorian age. In 'De juventute', for example, Thackeray observes how the 'old world' seems utterly divided from the new by the coming of the 'railroad': to those who cannot remember the 'prae-railroad world . . . [w]e who lived before railways, and survive out of the ancient world, are like Father Noah and his family out of the Ark' (*WMT* xii. 233). Thus, with a logic now even more familiar from the experience of later modernity, it is always the most recently outmoded fashions that belong, most irredeemably, to the past. Yet, at the same time, the temporal process of fashion is cyclical rather than linear in trajectory, and so remains curiously unchanging and repetitive in essence. Thackeray's representation of history articulates a similar doubleness, a sense of being compelled to erase the past, but predestined to repeat it in a different guise. His singular capacity as a cultural historian lies in his ability to reproduce these new subjective rhythms of experience – feelings of anachronism, obsolescence, innovation and modernity that indirectly reflect the objective historical character of his era.

Notes

INTRODUCTION: THE ANTIQUARY OF THE FUTURE

1. Charlotte Brontë, *Jane Eyre*, ed. Michael Mason (Harmondsworth: Penguin, 1996), 6–7.
2. *Selections from George Eliot's Letters*, ed. Gordon S. Haight (New Haven: Yale University Press, 1985), 174.
3. Anthony Trollope, *An Autobiography*, ed. Michael Sadleir and Frederick Page (Oxford: Oxford University Press, 1980), 243.
4. Henry James, *The Tragic Muse*, ed. Philip Horne (Harmondsworth: Penguin, 1995), 4.
5. Georg Lukács, *The Historical Novel*, trans. Hannah and Stanley Mitchell (London: Merlin Press, 1962), 201.
6. Geoffrey Tillotson, *Thackeray the Novelist* (Cambridge: Cambridge University Press, 1954), p. ix.
7. See Barbara Hardy, *The Exposure of Luxury: Radical Themes in Thackeray* (London: Peter Owen, 1972), 13; and John Carey, *Thackeray: Prodigal Genius* (London: Faber & Faber, 1977), 9.
8. See J. A. Sutherland, *Thackeray at Work* (London: Athlone Press, 1974), 1.
9. See Andrew Sanders, *The Victorian Historical Novel 1840–1880* (London: Macmillan, 1978), p. ix.
10. Trollope, *An Autobiography*, 41.
11. See Eve Kosofsky Sedgwick, *Between Men: English Literature and Male Homosocial Desire* (New York: Columbia University Press, 1985), 134–60 and *Epistemology of the Closet* (Harmondsworth: Penguin Books, 1994), 188–95; Patrick Brantlinger, *Rule of Darkness: British Literature and Imperialism, 1830–1914* (Ithaca, NY: Cornell University Press, 1988), 73–107; and Andrew H. Miller, *Novels behind Glass: Commodity Culture and Victorian Narrative* (Cambridge: Cambridge University Press, 1995), 14–19.
12. See Carey, *Thackeray*, 9–10.

CHAPTER 1. WRITING FOR THE DAY: THACKERAY AND THE LITERARY TRADE

1. J. W. Kaye, '*Pendennis* The Literary Profession', *North British Review*, 13/26 (Aug. 1850), 343.
2. See Margaret Beetham, 'Towards a Theory of the Periodical as a Publishing Genre' in Laurel Brake, Aled Jones and Lionel Madden (eds.), *Investigating Victorian Journalism* (Basingstoke: Macmillan, 1990), 19–20.
3. See Stephen Canham, 'Art and the Illustrations of *Vanity Fair* and *The Newcomes*' in Bill Katz (ed.), *A History of Book Illustration: 29 Points of View* (Metuchen, NJ: Scarecrow Press, 1994), 468.
4. See Douglas Jerrold (ed.), *Heads of the People: Or Portraits of the English, drawn by Kenny Meadows; With Original Essays by Distinguished Writers* (2 vols; London: Robert Tyas, 1840–1).
5. Edgar F. Harden, *The Emergence of Thackeray's Serial Fiction* (Athens, Ga: University of Georgia Press, 1979), 1–4.
6. Ibid. 25.
7. Geoffrey Tillotson, *Thackeray the Novelist* (Cambridge: Cambridge University Press, 1954), 15.
8. See Michel Foucault, 'What is an Author?', in *The Foucault Reader*, ed. Paul Rabinow (Harmondsworth: Penguin, 1986), 101–20.
9. See Simon Dentith, *Parody* (London: Routledge, 2000), 5–6.
10. Ibid. 77.
11. See Robert A. Colby, *Thackeray's Canvass of Humanity: An Author and his Public* (Columbus, Oh: Ohio State University Press, 1979), 213.
12. See Thomas Carlyle, 'Biography' (1832), in *Critical and Miscellaneous Essays, iii* (London: Chapman & Hall, 1888), 40.
13. See Thomas Carlyle, *On Heroes, Hero-Worship and the Heroic in History*, ed. Carl Niemeyer (Lincoln, Neb.: University of Nebraska Press, 1966), 154–95.

CHAPTER 2. ALLEGORY AND THE WORLD OF THINGS

1. John Carey, *Thackeray: Prodigal Genius* (London: Faber & Faber, 1977), 93.
2. On this point, see Pierre Bourdieu, *Distinction: A Social Critique of the Judgement of Taste*, trans. Richard Nice (London: Routledge, 1986), 485–94.
3. See Carey, *Thackeray*, 84–5.
4. George Orwell, 'Oysters and Brown Stout', in Sonia Orwell and Ian Angus (eds.), *The Collected Essays, Journalism and Letters of George Orwell. Volume III. As I Please. 1943–1945* (London: Secker & Warburg, 1968), 301.

5. Ibid. 300.
6. See Barbara Hardy, *The Exposure of Luxury: Radical Themes in Thackeray* (London: Peter Owen, 1972), 111, 20.
7. See Karl Marx, 'The Fetishism of the Commodity and its Secret', in *Capital: A Critique of Political Economy Volume One,* trans. Ben Fowkes (Harmondsworth: Penguin, 1976), 163–77.
8. See Carey, *Thackeray*, 61.
9. See Thomas Carlyle, *Past and Present*, ed. Richard D. Altick (New York: New York University Press, 1965), 147–51.
10. John Bunyan, *The Pilgrim's Progress from this World to That which is to Come*, ed. James Blanton Wharey (2nd. edn., Oxford: Oxford University Press, 1960), 88.
11. Walter Benjamin, *The Origin of German Tragic Drama*, trans. John Osborne (London: Verso, 1985), 223.
12. See Andrew H. Miller, *Novels behind Glass: Commodity Culture and Victorian Narrative* (Cambridge: Cambridge University Press, 1995), 18.
13. Karl Marx, *Selected Writings*, ed. David McClellan (Oxford: Oxford University Press, 1977), 224.
14. See Gary R. Dyer, 'The "Vanity Fair" of Nineteenth Century England: Commerce, Women, and the East in the Ladies' Bazaar', *Nineteenth-Century Literature*, 46/2 (1991), 201–12.
15. See Miller, *Novels behind Glass*, 50–3.
16. See Walter Benjamin, *Charles Baudelaire: A Lyric Poet in the Era of High Capitalism*, trans. Harry Zohn (London: Verso, 1983), 172.

CHAPTER 3. TRUTHFUL ILLUSIONS: THACKERAY'S REALISM

1. See Barbara Hardy, *The Exposure of Luxury: Radical Themes in Thackeray* (London: Peter Owen, 1972), 56; and Alison Byerly, *Realism, Representation, and the Arts in Nineteenth-Century Literature* (Cambridge: Cambridge University Press, 1997), 63–4.
2. See Henry James, *The House of Fiction: Essays on the Novel*, ed. with an introduction by Leon Edel (London: Mercury Books, 1962), 26.
3. See Jack P. Rawlins, *Thackeray's Novels: A Fiction that is True* (Berkeley and Los Angeles: University of California Press, 1974), 55.
4. See the opening of book IV chapter 1 in Henry Fielding, *The History of Tom Jones*, ed. R. P. C. Mutter (repr. Harmondsworth: Penguin, 1985), 119.
5. See Georg Lukács, *The Theory of the Novel: A Historico-Philosophical Essay on the Forms of Great Epic Literature*, trans. Anna Bostock (London: Merlin Press, 1971), 112–31.
6. See Robin Gilmour, *The Idea of the Gentleman in the Victorian Novel* (London: George Allen & Unwin, 1981), 76.

7. See R. D. McMaster, *Thackeray's Cultural Frame of Reference: Allusion in* The Newcomes (Houndmills: Macmillan, 1991), 100.
8. Eve Kosofsky Sedgwick, *Epistemology of the Closet* (Harmondsworth: Penguin, 1994), 193.
9. John Peck, 'Racism in the Mid-Victorian Novel: Thackeray's *Philip*' in Gary Day (ed.), *Varieties of Victorianism: The Uses of a Past* (Houndmills: Macmillan, 1998), 130.

CHAPTER 4. HISTORIOGRAPHY AND HISTORICAL FICTION

1. See Thomas Carlyle, *On Heroes, Hero-Worship and the Heroic in History*, ed. Carl Niemeyer (Lincoln, Neb.: University of Nebraska Press, 1966), 183.
2. See Georg Lukács, *The Historical Novel*, trans. Hannah and Stanley Mitchell (London: Merlin Press, 1962), 202–4.
3. See e.g. J. Hillis Miller, *Fiction and Repetition: Seven English Novels* (Oxford: Basil Blackwell, 1982), 78.
4. Eve Kosofsky Sedgwick, *Between Men: English Literature and Male Homosocial Desire* (New York: Columbia University Press, 1985), 146–7.
5. Ibid. 149–51.
6. See Catherine Peters, *Thackeray's Universe: Shifting Worlds of Imagination and Reality* (London: Faber & Faber, 1987), 202.
7. See Jack P. Rawlins, *Thackeray's Novels: A Fiction that is True* (Berkeley and Los Angeles: University of California Press, 1974), 192.
8. Andrew Sanders, *The Victorian Historical Novel, 1840–1880* (London: Macmillan, 1978), 20.
9. See Miller, *Fiction and Repetition*, 114.
10. See Wordsworth and Coleridge, *Lyrical Ballads*, ed. R. L. Brett and A.R. Jones (repr. London: Methuen, 1986), 266.
11. See Wordsworth, *The Prelude or Growth of a Poet's Mind*, ed. Ernest de Selincourt (Oxford: Oxford University Press, 1970), book XI, 213.
12. See John Carey, *Thackeray: Prodigal Genius* (London: Faber & Faber, 1977), 146–8.
13. See Walter Benjamin, 'Theses on the Philosophy of History', in *Illuminations*, ed. Hannah Arendt and trans. Harry Zohn (Bungay: Fontana/Collins, 1973), 259–60.
14. Carey, *Thackeray*, 130.

Select Bibliography

WORKS BY W. M. THACKERAY

Collected Editions

The Biographical Edition of The Works of William Makepeace Thackeray (13 vols.; London: Smith, Elder, & Co., 1898–9). Includes biographical introductions by Thackeray's daughter, Anne Ritchie.

The Oxford Thackeray, ed. George Saintsbury (17 vols.; London: Oxford University Press, 1908).

The Letters and Private Papers of William Makepeace Thackeray, ed. Gordon N. Ray (4 vols.; London: Oxford University Press, 1945–6).

The Works of W. M. Thackeray, ed. Peter L. Shillingsburg (7 vols. to date; New York and London: Garland Publishing/Ann Arbor: University of Michigan Press, 1989–). A modern scholarly edition of Thackeray's collected works, as yet incomplete.

The Letters and Private Papers of William Makepeace Thackeray (2 vols.; New York and London: Garland Publishing, 1994). A supplement to Gordon N. Ray's 1945–6 edition.

Separate Editions

N.B. Most of the works listed below are available in other paperback editions, though some choose to omit the illustrations that were often an indispensable element of the design of Thackeray's original texts.

Vanity Fair: A Novel without a Hero, ed. John Sutherland (Oxford: Oxford University Press, 1983). Includes Thackeray's illustrations for the original serial publication of the novel.

The Memoirs of Barry Lyndon, Esq., ed. Andrew Sanders (Oxford: Oxford University Press, 1984). Based on the revised and retitled text of 1856, but incorporating deleted material from the original 1844 edition.

The History of Henry Esmond, Esq., ed. Donald Hawes (Oxford: Oxford University Press, 1991).

A Shabby Genteel Story and Other Writings, ed. D. J. Taylor (London: Everyman, 1993). A modern anthology of some of Thackeray's early fictional tales and sketches.

The History of Pendennis, ed. John Sutherland (Oxford: Oxford University Press, 1994). Includes Thackeray's illustrations for the original serial publication of the novel.

The Newcomes:: Memoirs of a Most Respectable Family, ed. Andrew Sanders (Oxford: Oxford University Press, 1995). Includes illustrations by Richard Doyle for the original serial publication of the novel.

The Four Georges and The English Humourists (Phoenix Mill: Alan Sutton Publishing, 1995). An abridged edition of Thackeray's lecture series on the eighteenth century.

The Memoirs of Mr Charles J. Yellowplush (Phoenix Mill: Sutton Publishing, 1997).

CRITICAL AND BIOGRAPHICAL WORKS ON W. M. THACKERAY

Brantlinger, Patrick, *Rule of Darkness: British Literature and Imperialism, 1830–1914* (Ithaca, NY: Cornell University Press, 1988). See chapter 3, 'Thackeray's India'.

Byerly, Alison, *Realism, Representation, and the Arts in Nineteenth-Century Literature* (Cambridge: Cambridge University Press, 1997). See chapter 2 for a discussion of realism and theatricality in Thackeray's fiction.

Canham, Stephen, 'Art and the Illustrations of *Vanity Fair* and *The Newcomes*', in Bill Katz (ed.), *A History of Book Illustration: 29 Points of View* (Metuchen, NJ: Scarecrow Press, 1994), 462–87.

Carey, John, *Thackeray: Prodigal Genius* (London: Faber & Faber, 1977). A stimulating assessment, though dogmatically unsympathetic to later Thackeray.

Clarke, Micael M., *Thackeray and Women* (DeKalb, Ill.: Northern Illinois University Press, 1995).

Colby, Robert A., *Thackeray's Canvass of Humanity: An Author and his Public* (Columbus, Oh.: Ohio State University Press, 1979). An impressively documented study.

Dentith, Simon, *Parody* (London: Routledge, 2000). Chapter 3 includes Thackeray within a discussion of the relationship between parody and the form of the novel.

Douglas, Dennis, 'Thackeray and the Uses of History', *The Yearbook of English Studies, 5* (1975), 164–77.

Dyer, Gary R., 'The "Vanity Fair" of Nineteenth Century England: Commerce, Women, and the East in the Ladies' Bazaar', *Nineteenth-Century Literature, 46/2* (1991), 196–222. Useful for the nineteenth-century cultural context of Thackeray's novel.

Ferris, Ina, 'Realism and the Discord of Ending: The Example of Thackeray', *Nineteenth-Century Fiction*, 38/3 (1983), 289–303.

Fisher, Judith L., 'Image versus Text in the Illustrated Novels of William Makepeace Thackeray', in Carol T. Christ and John O. Jordan (eds.), *Victorian Literature and the Victorian Visual Imagination* (Berkeley and Los Angeles: University of California Press, 1995), 60–87.

Gilmour, Robin, *The Idea of the Gentleman in the Victorian Novel* (London: George Allen & Unwin, 1981). Contains extensive reference to Thackeray.

Harden, Edgar F., *The Emergence of Thackeray's Serial Fiction* (Athens, Ga.: University of Georgia Press, 1979).

Hardy, Barbara, *The Exposure of Luxury: Radical Themes in Thackeray* (London: Peter Owen, 1972).

Howes, Craig, '*Pendennis* and the Controversy on the "Dignity of Literature"', *Nineteenth-Century Literature*, 41 /3 (1986), 269–98.

Levine, George, *The Realistic Imagination: English Fiction from* Frankenstein *to* Lady Chatterley (Chicago: University of Chicago Press, 1983). See chapters 6–8 for a discussion of Thackeray, chiefly *Pendennis.*

Lukács, Georg, *The Historical Novel*, trans. Hannah and Stanley Mitchell (London: Merlin Press, 1962). A brief, but important, discussion of Thackeray's place within the fictional genre established by Scott.

Lund, Michael, *Reading Thackeray* (Detroit: Wayne State University Press, 1988). A critical study influenced by reader-response theory.

McCuskey, Brian, 'Fetishizing the Flunkey: Thackeray and the Uses of Deviance', *Novel*, 32/3 (1999), 384–400. An interesting discussion of Thackeray's representations of class and gender.

McMaster, Juliet, *Thackeray: The Major Novels* (Manchester: Manchester University Press, 1971).

McMaster, R. D., *Thackeray's Cultural Frame of Reference: Allusion in* The Newcomes (Houndmills: Macmillan, 1991).

Miller, Andrew H., *Novels behind Glass: Commodity Culture and Victorian Narrative* (Cambridge: Cambridge University Press, 1995). Chapter 2 contains a sophisticated reading of Thackeray, principally *Vanity Fair.*

Miller, J. Hillis, *Fiction and Repetition: Seven English Novels* (Oxford: Basil Blackwell, 1982). See chapter 4 on *Henry Esmond.*

Orwell, George, 'Oysters and Brown Stout', in *The Collected Essays, Journalism and Letters of George Orwell. Volume III. As I Please. 1943–1945*, ed. Sonia Orwell and Ian Angus (London: Secker & Warburg, 1968), pp. 299–302.

Pearson, Richard, *W. M. Thackeray and the Mediated Text: Writing for Periodicals in the Mid-Nineteenth Century* (Aldershot: Ashgate, 2000).

Peck, John, 'Racism in the Mid-Victorian Novel: Thackeray's *Philip*', in Gary Day (ed.), *Varieties of Victorianism: The Uses of a Past* (Houndmills: Macmillan, 1998), 126–41.

Peters, Catherine, *Thackeray's Universe: Shifting Worlds of Imagination and Reality* (London: Faber & Faber, 1987). A critical biography.

Pollard, Arthur (ed.), *Thackeray:* Vanity Fair. *A Casebook* (Houndmills: Macmillan, 1978). A collection of critical documents stretching from contemporary reviews to studies from the 1970s.

Prawer, S. S., *Breeches and Metaphysics: Thackeray's German Discourse* (Oxford: Legenda, 1997).

Rawlins, Jack P., *Thackeray's Novels: A Fiction that is True* (Berkeley and Los Angeles: University of California Press, 1974).

Ray, Gordon N., *Thackeray: The Uses of Adversity, 1811–1846* (London: Oxford University Press, 1955).

—— *Thackeray: The Age of Wisdom, 1847–1863* (London: Oxford University Press, 1958). Published in two volumes, this remains the most comprehensive biography.

Sanders, Andrew, *The Victorian Historical Novel* 1840–1880 (London: Macmillan, 1978). See chapter 5 on *Henry Esmond* and *The Virginians.*

Sedgwick, Eve Kosofsky, *Between Men: English Literature and Male Homosocial Desire* (New York: Columbia University Press, 1985). Chapter 8 contains an insightful reading of *Henry Esmond.*

—— *Epistemology of the Closet* (Harmondsworth: Penguin, 1994). Chapter 4 includes a discussion of the figure of the 'batchelor' and the space of 'bohemia' in Thackeray's later fiction.

Shillingsburg, Peter L., *Pegasus in Harness: Victorian Publishing and W.M. Thackeray* (Charlottesville, Va.: University Press of Virginia, 1992).

Sudrann, Jean, 'The Philosopher's Property'': Thackeray and the Use of Time', *Victorian Studies*, 10/4 (1967), 359–88.

Sutherland, J. A., *Thackeray at Work* (London: Athlone Press, 1974).

Taylor, D. J., *Thackeray* (London: Chatto & Windus, 1999). The most recent biography.

Thrall, Miriam M. H., *Rebellions Fraser's: No! Yorke's Magazine in the Days of Maginn, Thackeray, and Carlyle* (New York: Columbia University Press, 1934). A history of *Fraser's Magazine* focusing on the period in which Thackeray was one of its principal contributors.

Tillotson, Geoffrey, *Thackeray the Novelist* (Cambridge: Cambridge University Press, 1954). and Hawes, Donald (eds.), *Thackeray: The Critical Heritage* (London: Routledge and Kegan Paul, 1968). A valuable anthology of critical essays and reviews of Thackeray published during the nineteenth century.

Trollope, Anthony, *Thackeray* (London: Macmillan, 1895). One of the first critical biographies of Thackeray written by one of his most notable Victorian admirers.

Index

Addison, Joseph, 96
  The Campaign, 94
Ainsworth, William Harrison
  Jack Sheppard, 26

Balzac, Honore de, 4, 65, 67
  Illusions Perdues, 32
Beetham, Margaret, 15
Bell, Robert, 57–9
Benjamin, Walter, 50–1, 56, 107
Blackwood, John, 2
Blanchard, Laman, 16–7, 31
Bourdieu, Pierre, 44
Brantlinger, Patrick, 8
Brontë, Charlotte
  Jane Eyre, 1–2, 59
Bulwer-Lytton, Edward, 16–7, 23–4, 31, 33, 51
  Eugene Aram, 26
Bunyan, John
  The Pilgrim's Progress, 49–50
Byerly, Alison, 61
Byron, Lord, 31, 36

Calcutta Star, 13
Canham, Stephen, 18
Carey, John, 4, 10, 35, 39, 42, 106, 108
Carlyle, Thomas, 2, 29, 46–8, 64
  The French Revolution, 89
  'The Hero as Man of Letters', 32
Carmichael-Smyth, Henry, 13
Cervantes, Miguel de
  Don Quixote, 72–3
Constitutional, 13
Cooper, Fenimore, 24
Cornhill Magazine, 14–5, 83, 105

Dentith, Simon, 24–5
Dickens, Charles, 1–5, 15–66, 30, 33, 37, 42
  David Copperfield, 62–3, 71
  Great Expectations, 82
  Oliver Twist, 26
  Sketches by Bo:, 19
Disraeli, Benjamin, 24, 51
Dumas, Alexandre, 3, 103
Dyer, Gary, 55

Edinburgh Review, 7
Eliot, George, 1–2, 4–5, 63

Fielding, Henry, 7, 16, 37, 64, 84
  Tom Jones, 63, 73
Flaubert, Gustave, 4, 63
Foucault, Michel, 2(1
Frazer's Magazine, 6, 13–4, 16, 18, 21, 27, 35

Gaskell, Elizabeth, 42
Gilmour, Robin, 73
Goethe, Johann Wolfgang von
  The Sorrows of Young Werther, 31, 37
  Wilhelm Meister's Apprenticeship, 66
Gore, Catherine, 24–5

Harden, Edgar, 19
Hardy, Barbara, 4, 39, 61
Hardy, Thomas, 4

James, G.P.R., 24
James, Henry, 3, 63
  'The Art of Fiction', 61
Jerrold, Douglas
  Heads of the People, 18
Joyce, James
  Ulysses, 25

Kant, Immanuel, 36
Kaye, J.W., 13

Lever, Charles, 24
Confessions of Harty Lorrequer, 27
Lewes, G.H., 3, 59
Lukács, Georg, 4, 67, 90–1, 99

Macaulay, Thomas Babington, 96
History of England, 84
Maginn, William, 13
Masson, David, 62–3
Marx, Karl, 33, 41
(and Friedrich Engels) *The Communist Manifesto*, 53, 55
McMaster, R.D., 75
Michelet, Jules, 88
Miller, Andrew, 8, 52, 56
Miller, J. Hillis, 103
Montaigne, Michel de
Essays, 104
Morning Chronicle, 13, 30

National Standard, 13

Orwell, George, 4, 38

Peck, John, 82
Proust, Marcel, 106
Punch, 6, 14, 18, 20, 24, 36, 38, 46

Quarterly Review, 59

Rabelais, Francois, 37
Rawlins, Jack, 63, 100
Richardson, Samuel, 72
Rigby, Elizabeth, 59

Sanders, Andrew, 6, 102
Scott, Walter, 4, 6, 85–6, 105
Ivanhoe, 24
Waverley, 95–6, 98
Sedgwick, Eve Kosofsky, 8, 80–1, 96–7
Shakespeare, William, 16
Smith, Goldwin, 7
The Spectator, 72
Steele, Richard, 96
Sterne, Lawrence, 78
Sutherland, John, 6
Swift, Jonathan, 96

Thackeray, William Makepeace
The Adventures of Philip, 11, 17, 22, 50, 64, 66–7, 77–83, 85
'A Box of Novels', 16
'A Brother of the Press', 16, 20
Catherine, 6, 13, 26–9, 85
Christmas Books, 21
Comic Tales and Sketches, 18
Denis Duval, 6, 10, 102–3
'The Dignity of Literature', 30, 33
'A Dinner in the City', 36, 38
'The English Humourists of the Eighteenth Century', 34, 84
'The Fatal Boots', 40––1, 46
FitzBoodle's Confessions, 37
The Four Georges, 84, 86, 89–90
The History of Henry Esmond, 4–7, 11, 19, 22, 85, 87–8, 90–7, 99–105
The History of Pendennis, 3, 8–9, 11, 13, 22, 30–4, 62–71, 73, 77, 79–81, 85
'The History of Samuel Titmarsh and the Great Hoggarty Diamond', 40–2, 46
The Irish Sketch Book, 18
'A Little Dinner at Timmins's', 42–4, 52
Lovel the Widower, 77
The Luck of Barry Lyndon, 10, 13–4, 27–9, 85, 90, 92–3
The Memoirs of Mr. Charles J. Yellowplush, 16, 22–4
'Memorials of Gormandising', 35–7, 40
The Newcomes, 3–5, 11, 22, 64, 66–7, 71–7, 79–82, 85, 100
'On the Press and the Public', 20
The Paris Sketch Book, 18, 38
Punch's Prize Novelists, 24–5, 30
Rebecca and Rowena, 24
The Roundabout Papers, 14, 20, 35, 105–8
The Snobs of England, 14, 46–8
'Sorrows of Werther', 36
Vanity Fair, 1, 4–5, 8, 10–1, 17–9, 21, 39, 44–5, 49–62, 64–5, 67, 77, 85, 92
The Virginians, 4, 7, 11, 85, 92, 97–8, 100–03
Tillotson, Geoffrey, 4, 20
The Times, 13
Tolstoy, Leo, 3
Trollope, Anthony, 1, 7, 19, 61, 65, 73
An Autobiography, 2

Wordsworth, William, 31, 105–6
Lyrical Ballads, 104

Zola, Émile, 63